Yesterday's Town:
Bury St Edmunds 1992
has been published
in a Limited Edition
of which this is

Number

YESTERDAY'S TOWN:
BURY ST EDMUNDS

In 1910 the 2nd Battalion the Suffolk Regiment visited the town.
Townspeople crowd Risbygate Street as they join the troops for their
Sunday morning Church Parade. (JAW)

The Unitarian Meeting House, Churchgate Street, was originally built for the Presbyterians in 1711. This is one of the finest buildings in the town, and there can be few, if any, town meeting houses which surpass it. After years of neglect, it has recently been skilfully conserved. (ECN)

YESTERDAY'S TOWN:
BURY ST EDMUNDS

BY

MARGARET STATHAM

BARON
MCMXCII

PUBLISHED BY BARON BIRCH FOR QUOTES LIMITED
AND PRODUCED BY KEY COMPOSITION
CHENEY & SONS, SOUTH MIDLANDS
LITHOPLATES, RAVENPRINT AND
WBC BOOKBINDERS

ISBN 0 86023 516 5

CONTENTS

ACKNOWLEDGEMENTS

I must first of all thank Clive Birch, a friend as well as a publisher, who is publishing this book, undersubscribed as it is, in a period of recession. Without the 350 or so subscribers, this book would not have been possible, and I am deeply grateful to all of them for their support. Thanks are due, too, to the staff of Bury Central Library, the Bury Branch of the Record Office, Moyses Hall Museum and the Clock Museum, who kept the subscription files.

Much of my research had been done at the Bury St Edmunds Branch of the Suffolk Record Office, where the staff have been unfailing helpful. Over many years I have been fortunate enough to discuss Bury St Edmunds topics with many people. Although it is impossible to name them all, I do appreciate the value of discussion of this sort. Amanda Arrowsmith, Diarmaid McCulloch, Norman Scarfe, Michael Tupling and Stanley West have all been most helpful in various ways.

Those who have generously made illustrations available are indicated in the captions, but Joe Wakerley has made a very special contribution to the book by allowing me to use so many items from his collection of photographs of Bury St Edmunds.

My friend David Baynes-Cope has helped in all sorts of ways and, finally, I must thank my daughter, Helen, who always encourages me to continue with my work on the history of Bury, and is, I think, proud to have been born in Bury St Edmunds. I hope she likes her book.

ECN	E. C. Neser
St Eds	St Edmundsbury Borough Council Museum Service
JAW	J. A. Wakerley
DJE	D. J. Evans
MS	Margaret Statham
GFT	Guildhall Feoffment Trust
StE BC	St Edmundsbury Borough Council
OGJ	O. G. Jarman
BFP	*Bury Free Press*
LC	Lacy Scott
SRO(B)	Suffolk Record Office (Bury St Edmunds Branch)
PS	Paul Smith

FOREWORD

by the Very Reverend Raymond Furnell, Provost of St Edmundsbury

Once again Margaret Statham has brought 'Yesterday's Town' into today's consciousness, for here is an account of local history which weaves a rich and colourful pattern across the centuries.

In this book the reader's mind is stretched by the historical and sociological data, and the senses are encouraged, for in the descriptive passages the sight, sound and smell of the market places of St Mary's Square with its horse market, or Angel Hill with the colourful Bury Fair, all come alive.

While the book is concerned with yesteryear, there are those sections which have a remarkable familiarity for us in the last decade of the 20th century. Towards the end of the book, detailed reference is made to the town's benefactors, who always had an eye to the needs of the poor, both in body and spirit — a timely reminder perhaps to the reader.

There is a singularly tantalising side to this work; having taken us step by step through a particular period in our town's history, and expecting a neat conclusion, Margaret leaves the reader with a question — unanswered — perhaps forecasting another literary work from this prolific pen.

Having thoroughly enjoyed a good read, walking Bury streets will never be the same again.

Raymond Furnell

DEDICATION

For Helen

INTRODUCTION

Although Bury St Edmunds was not incorporated as a borough until 1606, it had been an urban place, and a large one, long before then. Imagine the 650-plus households living in the town in 1086 when the Domesday survey was compiled — that was no village. At the centre of the Liberty of St Edmund, and developing as a marketing and trading centre, it was surely what the geographers call a central place, servicing lesser communities in its hinterland.

Much detailed research on the history of Bury St Edmunds remains to be done, and many questions remain to be answered. The present state of the history of the town strikes me as being like a partially completed jig-saw puzzle. Some parts are coming on well, an attempt has been made with others, but perhaps the pieces are not all in the right place and, of course, there are lots of gaps, with a heap of unplaced pieces waiting on the edges to be fitted in. The lack of any considerable archaeological dimension is, I believe, a great handicap, and one hopes that not all the archaeological layers were destroyed when a large part of the west side of Cornhill, just within the line of the town wall and on the edge of the market place, was developed in the 1960s. Perhaps in years to come ever more sophisticated archaeological techniques will enable some of the most sensitive sites to be investigated with the archaeological equivalent of non-invasive surgery.

However, as the lack of archaeological investigation results almost entirely from the fact that the town escaped bombing during the war, and extensive central redevelopment after it, it does mean that there are a large number of historic buildings standing which are often much older than might be expected from a glance at the facade. A Victorian cottage in Cannon Street has recently revealed traces of a 13th century aisled construction within its relatively recent walls. It can be dangerous to take Bury St Edmunds at face value.

Work on the topographical evidence in the monastic cartularies will almost certainly produce additional information about the development of the town, and there will surely be something to be learned from the English Place-Name Society's Suffolk volume, which is now in preparation. Ms Moore has illuminated the operation of English medieval fairs, including that held at Bury. If the evidence can be found, it would be good to know more about the operation of the weekly markets, and the relationship between the town and the villages which provided many of the goods sold each week. Communication between town and the villages, presumably by carrier's cart, must also have been important. In one chaper I look, briefly, at some of the builders who have worked in Bury. Perhaps in future, research will provide more information about craftsmen capable of producing furniture such as the Clopton chairs.

There is really no end to the detailed studies that would help to complete the jig-saw puzzle picture of this town. It is a beautiful town, there are many things of great historical importance within it and, the more we know about it, the more intelligently and effectively can our heritage be conserved.

This drawing is described as 'The Departure of Captn. Poole from St Edmunds Bury on the 15th of October 1785. The Ascent of the Balloon was remarkably Fine & Gradual, and continu'd in View near an Hour, moving Eastward. The dot over the large tree in the View, shews the Proportionate appearance of the Balloon as seen from Angel Hill in Bury Fifty five Minutes after its Enlargement, at which time it was 20 Miles from Bury & 3 Miles from the surface of the Earth'. It is said locally that the buildings were drawn by Jacob Kendall, who published many local prints, while the figures were supplied by Henry William Bunbury, 1750-1811, the well known artist and caricaturist. It seems that each artist performed his task on a separate sheet of paper, and that the two were then stuck together — the join is just visible. Note the building on the left of the Abbey Gate, of which nothing is known, and also St Edmunds Hill, now Moreton Hall, on the top of the hill in the background, which was built for Professor John Symonds by Adam in 1773. (St Eds)

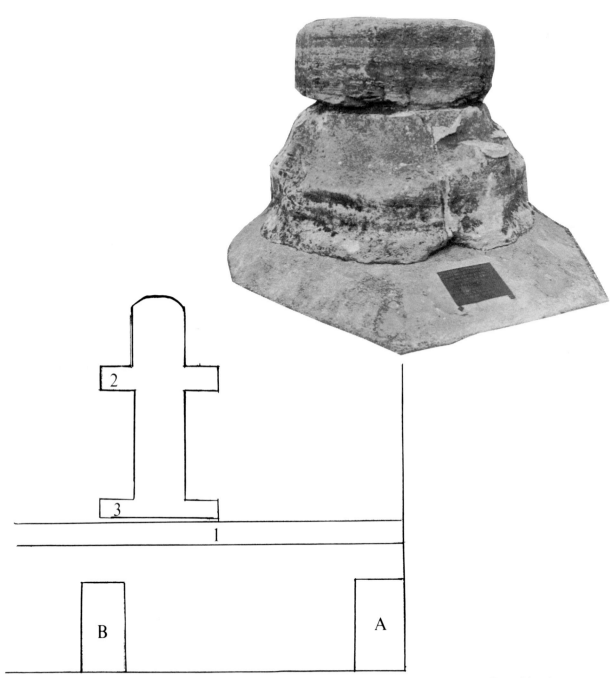

ABOVE: Known as the plague stone because, in times of epidemic, coins were dipped in vinegar placed in the cavity to attempt to ward off infection, this is really the base of the medieval St Peter's cross, one of four which marked the limits of the banleuca. It stood originally where Beetons Footpath meets Newmarket Road but now, after several moves, is sited in the grounds of the West Suffolk College, close to its original site. (MS)BELOW: Sketch plan to show possible westward extension of precinct under Abbot Baldwin. 1 Assumed line of roadway through later precinct which may have marked west boundary of Baldwin's precinct. 2 Site of pre-Conquest church of St Mary, demolished to make way for dextram brachiam of abbey church. 3 Site of Baldwin's church of St Denis, demolished to make way for north end of western transept. A St Mary's church. B St James's church.

BACK TO THE BEGINNING

It is believed that Sigeberht, king of the East Angles, founded a monastery at *Bedericesworth*, the first name given to the town, in about the year 630. The Abbey has yielded Ipswich-ware and the later Thetford-ware, which confirm the site was occupied then. So far, archaeologists have found no trace of Romano-British or pagan-Saxon settlement in today's town centre, although early Anglo-Saxon cemeteries and therefore settlements, did exist at Northumberland Avenue and Westgarth Gardens. These are now under housing estates on the outskirts of the historic town. Thus it appears that Sigeberht chose a new site for his monastery, perhaps on land which formed part of a Royal estate, for Abbo of Fleury, St Edmund's earliest biographer, believed that Bedericesworth was a Royal town.

The most significant event in the development of the town was the arrival of the remains of St Edmund, in about the year 900. After his death at the hands of the Danes in 869, Edmund had quickly been recognised as a saint and reports of miracles at his first burial place had begun to circulate. If *Bedericesworth* was an important Royal estate, it might explain why it was decided to remove St Edmund from his first burial place. An Anglo-Saxon charter credited another Edmund, who was King of the West Saxons from 939-946, with granting the land which surrounded the shrine to the saint, and those responsible for the shrine, in 945. Although the charter may have spurious elements, its boundary clause must have been written during the Anglo-Saxon period. It defined boundaries which remained those of the town until further land was taken in as a result of the West Suffolk Review Order of 1934. The area within the boundary defined in King Edmund's charter was called the *banleuca* and in medieval times its extent was marked by four stone crosses where the boundary crossed the roads into the town.

Dr Antonia Gransden has recently suggested that the Benedictines may have been introduced into *Bedericesworth* to replace the secular priests, who first cared for St Edmunds's relics, somewhat earlier than the traditional date during the reign of King Cnut, 1016-1035. The earliest life of St Edmund was written at Ramsey in Cambridgeshire between 985 and 987, and it is possible that St Oswald, the founder of Ramsey, who died in 992, may have had a hand in the introduction of the Benedictines to Bury. This might explain why the monks of Ramsey were interested in St Edmund. The tradition of the Abbey regarded King Cnut as founder of both Abbey and town. St Edmund was one of the English saints whose cults grew in the 1020s, which may have been a factor in the development of the town in the early 11th century as it recovered from devastation by the Danes. Soon after Cnut's stone church was dedicated in 1032, the town was known as Bury St Edmunds, and by 1066 it had its market and was the administrative centre for a mini-shire, known as the Liberty of St Edmund, comprising eight and a half hundreds (virtually the old administrative county of West Suffolk) given to the Abbey by King Edward the Confessor. The Confessor had also granted the abbot the right to have a mint, an indication of a stable urban community. 13

Domesday Book indicated that, in 1066, there were at least 310 men, many of whom would have been the head of a household, living in the town, which was valued at £10. By 1086 it was assessed at £20, two mills and two fishponds had appeared, and the town was said to be a league and a half in both length and breadth: about two and half miles in modern terms. In King William's time the built-up area covered much more land than before, because 342 houses had been built. Essential occupations such as bakers, brewers, tailors, shoemakers are mentioned — a thriving trading community.

The traditional view is that St Mary's Square formed the market place of pre-Conquest Bury St Edmunds, and that roads corresponding with the modern Northgate and Southgate Streets, with perhaps another to be equated with Westgate Street, converged there. The pre-Conquest town is envisaged as clustering round St Mary's Square, while Abbot Baldwin's new town is, according to this view, enshrined in the street-plan of the present town centre, with its market place in the Cornhill/Buttermarket area. Some documentary evidence suggests this is not the only explanation of the town centre's development. If the market had been moved before 1327, the traditional view may not hold good.

In recent years archaeologists have confirmed the long held theory that Northgate Street once continued across the precinct to join up with Sparhawk Street. Another investigation revealed signs of late-Saxon habitation on a site behind the Bury St Edmunds Branch of the Suffolk Record Office. Although the site of the St Edmunds Nursing Home was carefully monitored during building work, no trace of early settlement was found on that side of St Mary's Square. The burial place for *Bedericesworth* and, perhaps, early Bury St Edmunds also, may have been just east of this ancient road, for when Abbot Baldwin was building the church of St Denis (which stood where the north end of the west front of the abbey church was later built) large quantities of human bones were found, which were reverently placed in a wooden chapel dedicated to St Stephen. All known indications of early settlement within the town come from, and are close to, the Abbey precinct.

The thirteenth century *Gesta Sacristarum* states that Sacrists Ralph and Hervey, who were active during the time of Abbot Anselm between 1121 and 1148, were responsible for building the walls around the court of the Abbey, with their gates. It is probable that Anselm greatly enlarged the precinct because, when he had plans made for a much larger abbey church than that which Abbot Baldwin, 1065-1097/8, had intended, it became necessary to demolish, and replace on new sites, the two parish churches of the town. The old church of St Mary was in the way of the *dextram brachiam*, the right arm of the transept of Anselm's Abbey church. It was rebuilt in the south west corner of the precinct. The church of St Denis, which Abbot Baldwin had built, presumably for those who lived in his new town, was in the way of the north end of the western transept of Anselm's Abbey church. It, too, was demolished, and was replaced by a church dedicated to St James, on the site where the Cathedral is today. Both earlier churches had stood east of the ancient road, which once crossed the precinct, and which may well have marked the western boundary of Baldwin's precinct. If this is so, changes could well have been made to the town plan by incorporating a substantial area into the precinct.

Some writers have emphasised the importance of the great axis — the alignment of Churchgate Street with the archway through the Norman Tower leading into the precinct and with the great west door of the Abbey church — in the town plan. Others think this alignment was purely fortuitous. If Baldwin's precinct had to be enlarged to contain replacements for the two parish churches — and, for all we know, other monastic buildings — displaced by Anselm's grandiose plan, the streets leading to the main Abbey entrances could just as easily have formed part of a scheme laid out by Anselm as by Baldwin for his new town. Baldwin was a Frenchman, familiar with continental town plans, while Anselm was an Italian, a monk of Chiusi and abbot of St Saba at Rome before coming to England. He would have been familiar with the ruins of towns built on the grid plan favoured by the Romans. Streets, rather than a street, leading to the gates of the Abbey are suggested for the simple reason that Anselm's entrance gate was destroyed by rioting townsmen in 1327 and had to be replaced by the present Abbey Gate. That is not quite aligned with Abbeygate Street. With the town in revolt outside the Abbey, it would have been impracticable to pull down the old gate and rebuild on its site. The Norman gateway must surely have been repaired and kept in use   until   its elegant replacement was sufficiently advanced to keep out any intruders. If this is correct, the Abbeygate cannot be on the site of the Norman gate, so that could easily have stood just north of the present entrance, where it would have given a focal point at the end of Abbeygate Street.

The town, as well as the Abbey, had its defensible boundaries around the built-up area. William of Malmesbury stated that King Cnut had a ditch made to protect the town, while the *Gesta Sacristarum* says that Hervey, who was Sacrist from after 1121 until c1136, built the walls. The 12th century walls, which only extended from the West Gate to the North Gate, no doubt replaced earlier defensive banks and ditches on the western boundary. On other sides, Bury was surrounded by the river and marshy ground cut by numerous ditches and no attempt was made to extend the walls there. It is likely that the area within the walls grew with the town. When Dr West excavated the medieval bridge over the Linnet in Southgate Street near Maynewater Lane, there were remains of a flint wall on the north bank of the river. This could have been part of an earlier system of defence before an extension was made to include that part of Southgate Street which lies south of Maynewater Lane. It certainly looks very much like an early suburb, included later with the defended area. It is worth pondering on the names of the two late medieval suburbs of Bury, Eastgate Street and Risbygate Street; both stood entirely outside the gates from which they took their names, and Southgate Street has every appearance of a suburb outside an earlier line of town defences. Perhaps Northgate and Westgate Streets had similar origins as streets outside the gates from which they are named.

Guildhall Street, the West side of Cornhill and St John's Street were intra-mural streets, providing access to the walls, while St Andrews Street, the extra-mural roadway, was long known by such names as Ditchway, the Western Ditches or the Back Side, all of which reflect its relationship with the town wall. It looks as if the walls were in poor repair by 1478-1479. By the early sixteenth century the wills of townsmen whose houses adjoined the town wall often refer to access through it, to gardens or business premises outside. These breaches were not made at whim, but with formal consent, as when a lease from the Abbot and Convent to William Copping, fuller, made in 1527, gave permission for a gate to be made through the stone wall to the embankment beyond.

Medieval Bury St Edmunds had its own planning controls. In about 1191, Herbert the Dean, without prior consent, had put up a windmill on the Haberdon, but Abbot Samson would not allow it to remain. If the townsmen had ground their corn at Herbert's mill it would have reduced the Abbot's income from fees paid when the townsmen ground their corn at his mill. When Samson was considering this case, he observed that not even the King or a Royal judge could alter or build anything within the *banleuca* without consent.

Deeds from Abbot Samson's time give some details of property early on. One, dated to c1182-1200, concerned a plot before the great gate of the cemetery, granted to John the cook, which was only 20 feet long by 15 feeet wide and was held from the Sacrist for 6d a year. Another of Samson's deeds concerned the land of Richard of Horringer, which was before the great gate of the church of St Edmund. Its rent was 2s a year to the Sacrist and a shilling to the new Hospital , Abbot Samson's foundation at Babwell, St Saviour's. From a slightly later period, c1200-1211, another related to a shop and land of Thomas the goldsmith, the son of Ralph. This, too, was in front of the Great Gate of the monastery at the head of the stone house which belonged to Richard of Horringer. The grant also included all the land behind the stone wall which had belonged to Richard of Horringer 'from his shop to the road leading to *le Motstowe* [Angel Hill] right in front of [*perante*] the house of Ralph Valens and stretching as far as the land which the same Ralph holds of the Sacrist in the place which is called Paddocpol'. A grant of c1200-1211 gave Alan Mader and Alice his wife land and stone buildings which had belonged to John the mason and were near the west gate of the cemetery of St Edmunds (the Norman Tower). That land was between the land of Ralph of Stowe and Adam the Priest of Pakenham and was held for 3s a year to the Sacrist. The charter also indicated that two farthings each year were to be paid to the town Reeve, the standard payment of a halfpenny *hadgovel* rent which was charged for burgages in Bury St Edmunds.

These deeds raise interesting points, not least the use of stone as a building material. Building work must have continued almost without ceasing within the Abbey precinct and masons working on the Abbey church and conventual buildings no doubt undertook other work. It is probable that John the mason, to whom Samson granted land, would have been the master mason at the Abbey, probably working on the western towers, which were finished during Samson's abbacy. In Jocelin of Brakelond's *Chronicle of the Abbey of St Edmund* there are literary references to building houses of stone at this very time. Soon after 1196-7, the London merchants threatened to pull down some stone houses which Samson had built, for they were aggrieved that the Reeves had charged 15d on the waggons which came through the town on the way from Yarmouth, laden with herrings for the capital.

Abbot Samson gave some stone houses to the schoolmaster so that in future scholars would not have to pay for their accommodation. Jocelin does not tell us where these were but perhaps they were in Schoolhall Street (Honey Hill or Raingate Street) and formed part of the grammar school site, which later became Shire Hall.

A deed dating from 1182-1200 recorded that the townsmen, at their own cost, bought land in the market place which had belonged to Fredo the tanner. They built a stone house there from which to meet the annual rent of 24 shillings, for which they compounded *rep silver,* which they had formerly given to the Cellarer instead of reaping his crops and putting their cows to graze on his pastures.

Moyses Hall dates from this period and other houses which still retain traces of Norman stone work are known; more are being discovered. Norman House in Guildhall Street has some Norman arcading, and its stone plinth is easily seen. A Norman fireplace, which experts believe to be *in situ,* was revealed when Langton Place, between Hatter Street and Whiting Street, was created, and stone was used in other buildings in Hatter Street; it was sometimes called Heathenmans street, as it was the Jewry of medieval Bury St Edmunds until Abbot Samson expelled the Jews in 1190. Extra security requirements may explain why this street seems to have more than its fair share of early stone-built houses. A number of stone houses are mentioned in the Sacrist's rental of 1433, and presumably more would be found upon examining rentals of the estates of the other obedientiaries. It is also worth considering whether 'chantries' marked by Thomas Warren on his map of 1747 indicated properties which were at least partly built of stone. Most early buildings in Bury St Edmunds were, or course, built of timber. All would have been vulnerable to fire, and some of the earliest may well have been flimsy.

A serious fire in 1215 is mentioned in *The Bury St Edmunds Chronicle.* A third of the town was destroyed and this may well have stimulated redevelopment. Although, no doubt, large numbers of temporary structures were put up each year, the great international trading fair, which was held between the eve of St Edmund (19 November) and Christmas Eve during the high middle ages, may also have affected the town layout.

Bury St Edmunds as we know it today can be readily recognised in documents surviving from the second half of the thirteenth century but, as most were drawn up by the Abbey, references to other landowners were incidental. St Edmund's Abbey had such an overwhelming influence that it is all too easy to forget there were other landowners, some of them powerful men. There was the manor of Maidwater within the town, which was part of the Honour of Clare. It is probable that the nucleus of this estate was near the pool — which seems to be a widening of the river Linnet — called the Maidwater, which is shown on old maps, on the west side of what is now called Maynewater Lane. It is tempting to suppose that some of the Earl of Clare's land was in or near the present Friar's Lane, for the house of Clare was a great champion of the Franciscans. It would have been as likely as anyone to provide them with a site in the difficult, early stages of their attempt to establish themselves here. In 1238 Hawisia, Countess of Oxford, granted them a site, but Otto, Papal Legate, judged that neither the Friars Minor nor the Preaching Friars were entitled to settle within Bury. On 12 June 1258 the Friars Minor said mass in the house of Sir Roger de Harbridge, knight, on the east side of the North Gate but, while they were having dinner, the Friars' oratory and all their buildings were totally demolished. Eventually, after over five years at a site in Friars Lane, which is close to the Maid Water, it was finally agreed on 19 November 1263 that they should have their house in the extra-parochial area of Babwell. The Priory Hotel now stands on their site. Duke Richard of York had land in this area, with some of which he endowed the Friars in 1447; perhaps his predecessors also had land in this part of the town on which the Friars could have settled.

A tax assessment made in 1295, which is often called the 1295 Rental, gives an account of the property here which belonged to the obedientiaries of the Abbey. (The obedientiaries were the departmental heads of the various offices within the Abbey, such as the Sacrist, who was responsible for the services in the church, as well as being lord of Bury St Edmunds; the Precentor, who was in charge of the music and the Cellarer, who looked after the catering.) The assessment is arranged by wards, and first lists, street by street, the tenements, gardens, granges and curtilages which the officers of the Abbey owned. Once the house property in each ward had been listed, agricultural land in the town fields was described, and the document concluded with lists of the endowments of the Hospitals of St Peter, St Nicholas and Maison Dieu, *alias* St Petronilla.

The streets described are those which were within the walls of the town, plus its two medieval suburbs, Eastgate and Risbygate. Almost all can be identified with certainty, although many of the names have changed. Sometimes the description of land includes names still familiar today. The Cellarer, for instance, had 31 acres in the South Field which were called Nomans Meadows, as well as Hardwick Wood and Heath. Woods called Eastlee and Southlee, which belonged to the Sacrist, were in the Nowton Road area, and he also had the manor of Haberdon, which comprised 51½ acres with a mill. The house belonging to Haberdon was in Yoxfore Lane, which seems to be the modern St Botolph's Lane. Two tables set out the land of the various obedientiaries as shown in the 1295 assessment, and in a draft list of those in the town required to pay tax on land in 1340. The latter gives a somewhat higher acreage belonging to the obedientiaries than the 1295 list. It could be that woodland is included in the 1340 total, otherwise a modest addition had been made to the Abbey's holdings between 1295 and 1340. Many of the townsmen who held land would no doubt be exempt from the tax, but other taxpayers in 1340 had holdings amounting to more than 833 acres.

Much former monastic land came on the market after the dissolution of the Abbey in 1539. On 12 September 1544 King Henry VIII granted to John Eyer, Receiver General in the County of Suffolk — one of those who profited by the patronage of Sir Nicholas Bacon, the Lord Keeper of the Great Seal — over fifty parcels of former monastic property, some of which comprised a number of buildings or pieces of land. Eyer was also granted the right to collect the *hadgovel* rents, the ancient rents payable to the Sacrist for burgages in the town, probably by then already muddled with other, old customary payments. In connection with this, he obviously became the owner of the 1433 rental of the Sacrist's properties, which must have been used as the basis for his own records, to enable him to collect what was due. A garden in Eastgate Street, on which there had once been buildings, which had formerly belonged to the Prior of Thetford, also formed part of this grant. These, with some other former monastic property in Cambridgeshire, Norfolk and Essex, cost him £675 8s 10d, while he was granted further properties in Surrey and Essex for which he paid another £620. By and large the details given in Eyer's grant are insufficient to identify individual properties but, by working with other related documents, a picture emerges. Perhaps the most notable of Eyer's acquisitions so far identified was the Greyhound Inn, now the Suffolk Hotel. Other former monastic properties were granted to John and Andrew Manfield in 1546-7, to Thomas Bacon, citizen and salter of London, during the reign of Edward VI, to Thomas Andrews in 1561-2, to someone named Kett in 1564-5, to Christopher Hatton Esq, in 1571-2, and to Robert, Earl of Leicester in 1573-4. At the dissolution some of the Abbey's properties were subject to leases which still had years to run, while the Crown granted new leases after the dissolution.

Eyer soon sold off much of this property. It provided an opportunity for those with means to acquire adjacent sites and provide themselves with substantial houses. The Heigham family's house was at the corner of Crown Street and Westgate Street; they had long held this site from the Abbey but were now able to acquire it, with other nearby property. Eyer's nephew, Thomas Badby, amalgamated five plots in Mustowe to provide one substantial residence, and four out of five properties in Sparhawk Street were conveyed to Eyer and resold. The street was largely, if not entirely, redeveloped between 1539 and 1580.

A deed relating to some of the transfers involving these properties has survived among the records of the Guildhall Feoffees. On 7 October 1548, Eyer conveyed some of the properties he had acquired to Nicholas Plat, citizen and salter of London, who settled in Bury St Edmunds after he bought the Angel from Sir Thomas Jermyn. On 8 December 1550 some, perhaps all, of what Plat had purchased from Eyer was conveyed to William Tassell for £48 4s 2d. The property consisted of three small messuages or tenements with a garden in Raingate Street, a messuage or tenement with a garden in Southgate Street, two messuages or tenements in Crown Street, one of which abutted onto St Mary's church, a stable and garden in Punch (Athenaeum) Lane, a messuage or tenement in Churchgate Street, land in Maydewater (Maynewater) Lane, the 'Bores Hede' in Mustowe (Angel Hill or Mustow Street), a garden, and a stable with a garden adjoining, both in Brentgovel Street, three messuages in Longbrackland, land in Northgate Street, a messuage in Risbygate Street and a garden or orchard next to Teyfen.

The innate conservatism of the Abbey of St Edmund may well have inhibited the development of property in the town prior to the dissolution, and further work will no doubt reveal more examples of post-dissolution activity in the property market and in redevelopment.

LEFT: This pre-1919 photograph of Churchgate Street, taken through the arch of the Norman Tower, shows how the street is aligned with the archway. (JAW) Compare this with RIGHT: 1930s view, through the archway of the Abbeygate, which shows Abbeygate Street a little to the right. If the original 12th century gateway into the Abbey Court had survived, it might well have been aligned with Abbeygate Street. (JAW) BELOW: The East Gate, with the Fox Inn beside it, from Yates' Antiquities (1805), but probably based on an earlier print; the Corporation ordered all the five gates to be demolished in 1761. (MS) RIGHT: No picture is known of the South Gate, but Yates reproduced this engraving of the arms of the Abbey, the shield later granted to the town, which were formerly on it. (MS)

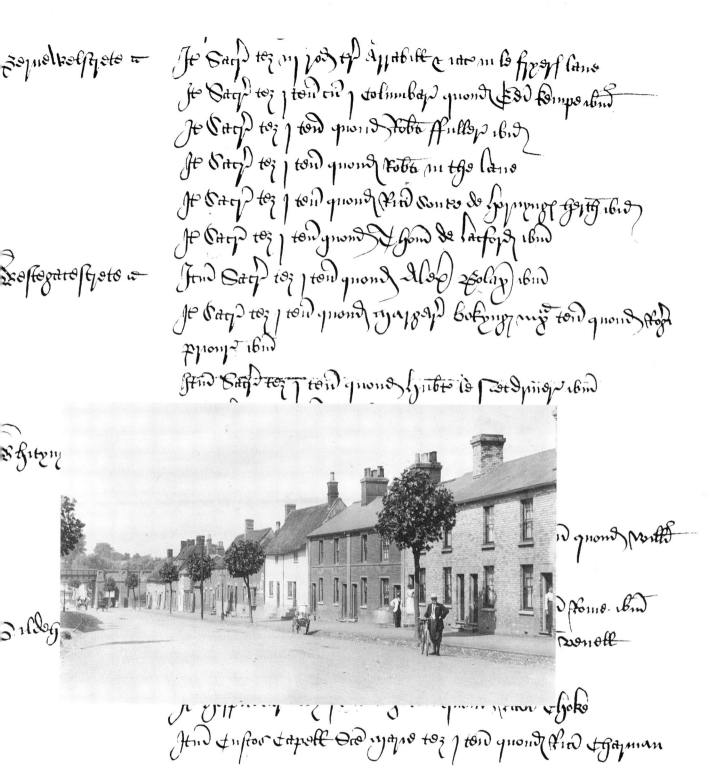

Part of the tax assessment made in 1295, from a later copy among the Borough archives. The Chronicle of Bury St Edmunds conveys the indignation felt by the Abbey as the Royal tax assessors sat in the Toll House to assess the town, although it was eventually agreed that this should not in future prejudice their rights. (St EBC at SRO(B)) INSET: East Ward: Eastgate Street, looking towards Angel Hill, before 1904. The bridge carrying the A45 over the street has replaced the railway bridge. (JAW)

ABOVE: Eastgate Street, from the other side of the railway bridge, but still looking towards Angel Hill; flags and bunting decorate many buildings, but why is not clear. The Ancient House, on the corner of Barn Lane, was then Ridley & Hooper's tannery. Before March 1907. (JAW) BELOW: The Ancient House during the 1930s, was a private house. From 1550 until 1665, this building was the Schoolhall, the first home of King Edward's Grammar School. Some timbers have been exposed on the Barn Lane side. (JAW)

ABOVE: The river Lark in flood at Eastgate Bridge, before 1907. (JAW) BELOW: The Fox Inn, viewed from the footbridge over the river, during the 1930s; when the Grammar School Governors were looking for a new home for the School, before they decided to build it in Northgate Street, they considered buying the Fox Inn and converting it. (JAW)

Bird's eye view of Bury St Edmunds, c1842; unsigned, on stylistic grounds it may be by Samuel Read. It shows St John's Church, which was consecrated in 1842, but the Guildhall Feoffment School, opened in 1843, seems to have been copied from the published architect's impression rather than the building itself. The unrestored Norman Tower, with the cupola on top and buildings butting against it on either side is shown. Note how spacious the Great Churchyard seems with only the two old avenues of trees — not a single tree can be seen between Clopton's Hospital, now the Provost's House, and Shire Hall, shown here before it was rebuilt in 1907. Facing Clopton's Hospital across the Churchyard is the Manor House where, from 1993, this remarkable picture will be displayed with other items from the St Edmundsbury Borough Council's art collections. How delightful it looks with its garden at the back, rather than a car park. The market area is clearly drawn. The Market Cross

had already been altered, by closing in the ground floor, to convert it into a Town Hall. Beside it is the Corn Exchange of 1836, altered to become the provision market when the Corn Exchange was opened in 1862, then the School of Art and Fire Station, later the Public Library; it has lately been converted into shops. The shambles, which used to stand on the site where the Corn Exchange was later built is shown here, together with inns, like the Bell, which surrounded the Market Place. Moyses Hall is easily recognised, as is Oakes & Bevan's Bank (now Lloyds). The Gaol in Sicklesmere Road, the Suffolk General Hospital and the Gas Works can be identified. One extraordinary feature is the east face of the Subscription Rooms, now the Athenaeum, shown here with classical columns. (St Eds)

ABOVE: *Oak House, 30 Eastgate Street, adjoining the Fox, was built with old timbers salvaged from the buildings demolished when Mustow Street was widened in 1926 — here before 1935. (JAW)*
BELOW: *This photograph, taken from some elevated position, in the first decade of this century, shows how the wide open space narrowed into the present Mustow Street, which had not been widened when this view was taken. (JAW)*

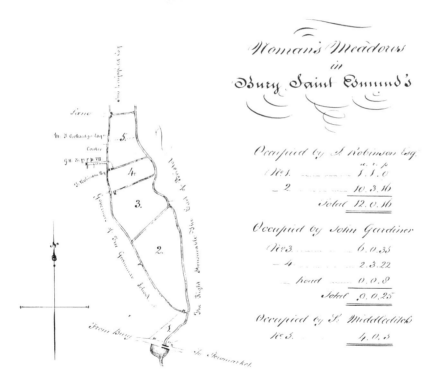

LEFT: A major land-owner in the East Ward in 1295 was the Hospital of St Nicholas, which stood well away from the built-up area, where Eastgate Street now divides into Hollow Road and Barton Road. Some of the buildings were converted into a dwelling house in the 16th century, and early in the 19th century it was the home of Philip Bennet of Rougham, who moved a window (JAW) RIGHT: from St Petronilla's Hospital, which used to stand near the Southgate, into the ruins of part of a building at St Nicholas. (JAW) BELOW: The South Ward: plan of Noman's Meadows, 1822, by J. G. Lenny; they had come into the possession of the Guildhall Feoffees under the Bury St Edmunds Enclosure Award of 1815. (GFT)

27

LEFT: The east side of Angel Hill, between the Abbey Gate and the Norman Tower, was called Goldsmiths Street with Glovers Street. This photograph was taken after Greene King's new brewhouse had been built; the first mash was in January 1939. It shows the west end of the Cathedral, before it was extended. Robert Lofts & Sons, high-class decorators, plumbers and sanitary engineers, then used the building which is now the Cathedral Shop. (JAW) RIGHT: This narrow section of what is now the Cathedral Shop illustrates the tiny dimensions of many properties of medieval origin. (MS) BELOW: Honey Hill is a relatively modern name, first found in Warren's map of 1747. The old name was Schoolhall Street, for the medieval song school was just east of St Mary's Church and the monastic grammar school stood on the site of Shire Hall. This photograph from the 1930s shows the former Coach and Horses (then a Wells and Winch house) with a brick front and round-headed doors. Next to it, 5 Honey Hill, with the Manor House, glimpsed on the right, are to become the headquarters of the St Edmundsbury Borough Council's Museum Service in 1993. (JAW)

ABOVE: St Mary's Square is often said to have been the pre-Conquest market place of Bury St Edmunds. On the right is part of St Mary's Vicarage which, with nos 5 and 6, may well be the work of Francis Sandys, the architect of Ickworth. (MS) BELOW: Many changes have taken place in this part of the west side of Southgate Street since this 1930s photograph. The house on the left has had its sash windows replaced and been plastered over. The two cottages have been demolished and replaced by a small house and an entrance into the back of the refurbished jettied house (which had a gallery at the back). Two modern houses have been built where there appears to have been a garden. The next house was a shop, with a good shop front, lost in renovation. The two houses at the end of the street are still there, modernised. (JAW)

ABOVE: On the opposite side of Southgate Street, the shop on the left (c1935) is now a private house, but the premises of R. J. Gooch, builder and undertaker, and the remaining houses, were demolished to make way for Alicia Court. (JAW) BELOW: Southgate Street at the turn of the century: on the right is the former Sword in Hand with old cottages on the left. Beyond is a building which looks as though it was a smithy, with the former Plough in the distance. (DJE)

ABOVE: A similar view of the Southgate Street cottages, of which the three nearest the camera are now a house known as Weavers' Rest. Timbers which had formerly been plastered over had been exposed before this photograph was taken in the 1930s. (JAW) BELOW: This view of Sparhawk Street probably dates from the 1920s. The flint building on the right has disappeared and flats have been built in its place; otherwise the scene is little changed. (JAW)

ABOVE: Hardwick Heath which in 1295 formed part of the estate of the Cellarer of the Abbey of St Edmund, is now an open space, providing recreational facilities for those living on nearby housing estates built in recent years. (MS) BELOW: West Ward: Hatter Street looked like this in the first decade of the century. Langton Place, linking Hatter Street and Whiting Street, has been cut through where the tree is here. Across Churchgate Street it continued as Bernewelstrete, and then took in land in Friars Lane. (JAW)

ABOVE: Guildhall Street before 1905; apart from costumes and the trap and baby carriage, this photograph could almost be taken today. (JAW) LEFT: Hatter Street was long ago called Heathenmans Street because it was the Jewry of medieval Bury. Several houses in the street retain early stone work, perhaps reflecting a need for greater security than was normally needed in its early days. When Langton Place was built, this fireplace, believed by experts to be in situ, was discovered in the side wall of the restaurant called Somewhere Else. (MS) RIGHT: These houses are on the east side of the Guildhall Street, near the Westgate Street end; Turret Close can be seen in the background; c1935. (JAW)

LEFT: These cottages are in Out Westgate c1935, which was not at all built in 1295. (JAW) RIGHT: Risbygate Ward: this building in Risbygate Street is scheduled as an Ancient Monument, although there are people who remember it taking its present form in the 1930s. It does look very new in this photograph, taken during that decade. (JAW) BELOW: Risbygate Street from near the Grapes Hotel. The house on the right of the picture was demolished in the 1950s to improve the corner. (JAW)

ABOVE: This photograph of St Johns Street shows the old Bury St Edmunds Police Station of 1892. Next to it is the premises which are Copelands, part of which has been cut through to make an entrance to Sergeants Walk, where the Bury Central Library was built behind the old Police Station in 1983. Nearer the camera, a building has been demolished and replaced by Apollo Travel's office. (JAW) BELOW: The only part of Abbeygate Street mentioned in 1295 was Barbour Rowe, but that need mean no more than that none of the obedientiaries had property elsewhere in the street. Olivers, whose 1950s trade card shows a commendable pride in trading from an historic building, was in the part known as Spicer Row. (JAW)

ABOVE: North Ward — the former County School in Northgate Street, before the extension was built in 1907. (JAW) BELOW: A little further along Northgate Street the houses on the left are still there, but some on the right have been lost where North Court is now. (JAW)

ABOVE: Still on the same side of the street, but now not far from the roundabout, is an old jettied house. This photograph shows part of the old SAPPA building (houses have recently been built on the site), and a sign for the United Yeast Company; c1935. (JAW) BELOW: Northgate Street from Pump Lane to Angel Hill once had an alternative name, High Street, which may well indicate that once it was the town's main shopping street. The fine houses include Northgate House, of which the garden front is shown, home to a number of notable Bury families, including Norah Lofts, the novelist. (JAW)

LEFT: The jettied house on the corner of Looms Lane was demolished in the 1960s to improve a difficult corner. The house next door retains many interesting features and beyond that is a little of the street front of Northgate House; c1935. (JAW) BELOW: Churchgate Street is mentioned in the 1295 assessment only as an abuttal of property on the corner of Athenaeum Lane. There have been few changes in this photograph taken, as usual, looking towards the Norman Tower, before 1912. (JAW) RIGHT: Crown Street is not mentioned in the 1295 assessment, though it may well have existed at Churchgovel Street. This photograph dates from 1864, before the cottages next to St Mary's were demolished, but after St James's Church had its pitched roof. The red brick houses had not yet replaced the old ones visible after the space where the almshouses had stood until 1813. (JAW)

ABOVE: Chequer Square is quite a modern name, but the area appears at an early date as Paddock Pool. It has been dominated by the Norman Tower since the time of Abbot Anselm, 1121-1148. (JAW) BELOW: Angel Lane appears from the 15th century under a variety of names. Many of the stables and coach houses recorded by Payne have become lock-up garages. (MS)

St Saviour's Hospital, founded by Abbot Samson, was built at Babwell, an extra-parochial place just on the northern boundary of Bury. The engraving is from Yates' Antiquities. (MS)

40

PAYNE'S 1833 TOWN

Richard Payne's survey of Bury St Edmunds, which he made in 1833, describes the town in minute detail just as it was at last about to expand out of the historic heart of the place, as ever more and more building land was required to provide homes for an increasing population. Payne went up and down each street, parish by parish, noting the name of each householder, describing the properties he found, giving the name of its owner and, in the case of the more extensive holdings, its area as well.

All the streets which Payne described were to be found in medieval rentals and surveys, but not all of them were then residential streets — St Andrews Street is a case in point. For the first time we can get a real feel of the different type of street in various parts of the town. Payne's work shows every sign of being carefully carried out, but two omissions have been noted. These are Clopton's Hospital, in the Churchyard, and the Gas Works, in Tayfen Road, although both are clearly marked on the plan of the town which he published in the following year.

The historic streets in the town centre had by 1833 become heavily built up. By 1831 the population was 11,436 of which 5,942 people lived in St James' parish and 5,494 in St Mary's. In the previous decade the population had risen from 9,999 and of the 1,437 additional residents, 1,173 were living in St James' parish. Throughout the town, homes for these people had been found by building courts, yards or squares, often on what had previously been detached gardens. A typical Bury court was built at right-angles to the street, and such housing was often clustered around a common yard, though in some cases there was some garden ground. By no means all these courts and yards had names. The only entirely new street which can be identified is Prospect Row, which appeared as St Edmunds Place on Lenny's map of 1823 and was called Prospect Row by Payne. Deeds of nearby property suggest that it was newly built at that time.

The ownership of property throughout Bury St Edmunds is revealed by Payne's survey, and William Steggles owned far more houses than even the Guildhall Feoffment Trust or the Corporation. Owner-occupiers were not often found then. Whereas those who live in the town centre today try to find a lock-up garage, their counterparts in the early 19th century were renting stables and hay lofts near their houses to accommodate their horses, chaises or coaches.

In Risbygate Street Payne noted properties, which were demolished to make way for Parkway, owned by someone called Lambert, whose name was given to Lambert's Row. In addition to residential property there were two malt offices and a bake office just before the Rising Sun Inn. Nearer to the town centre, on the north side of the street, was a waggon office, which probably stood where today there is a row of Victorian houses, set a little back from the street.

Out Risbygate began at the Chalk Road turn and land on the south side of the road belonged to George Brown, whose name was given to Queens and York Roads when they were first built and were known as Upper and Lower Brown Road. George Brown owned another waggon office, which was probably sited in the building Payne shows on the western corner of Spring Lane. There was a market garden on the ground were Victoria and Albert Streets were later built.

Chalk Lane was called Waterloo Street on Lenny's map of 1823 and a row of cottages stood there, before they were demolished in the 1960s, with a stone inscribed 'Waterloo Terrace 1815'. Chalk Lane had long existed as a way from Risbygate Street to Field Lane, but very probably there were few if any houses there until the terrace was built at the time of Waterloo, and an unsuccessful attempt was made to change an old name. Payne recorded a lime kiln here. Field Lane became Cemetery Road after the Cemetery was opened in 1855 and was again changed to Kings Road, to mark the Coronation of King George V in 1911. On the north side, near Chalk Lane, was the Cricket Ground, which was acquired by the Corporation in 1843 and is now a car park. Also on the north side, in addition to houses, there were a hat manufactory, a pig sty, a cow house, four bake-offices, two workshops and a mill, which stood just west of the Chalk Lane turn. The other side of Field Lane formed part of St Mary's parish.

St Andrews Street comes next, from which a large area had already been taken for the Cattle Market. Here were three cow-houses, a slaughter-house, a parchment maker's office, chandler's office, coachmaker's shop, a carver and gilder's workshop, a smithy, a granary and a weighing bridge. Fifteen gardens enclosed from the road, each containing 3r 0p, and which can be seen on the map, must have had their origins in something to do with the town's defences.

Much of Long Brackland was renamed St John's Street after the consecration of St John's church in 1842. The Quaker Meeting House was already there and Payne noted the following businesses: four bake-offices, a fellmonger, a wheelwright, a slaughter-house, malt office, a tailor, grocer, cornchandler, cook, a brew house, which was not attached to any pub or the like, a malt office and six unspecified workshops.

Short Brackland then continued to include Cannon Street as well, and Steggles had already built Cannon Place which consisted of 23 houses, one of which was a shop and another a bakery, lately the Chalice restaurant. On the west side of Pea Porridge Green, as the open space was then called, was the Dolphin public house, with its granary and cow house, and a windmill beside it.

In 1833 Northgate Street extended as far as the Tollgate Inn, including the present Fornham Road, although most of the houses were near the town centre. The Grammar School was in the building now known as St Michael's Close, and the Headmaster had his stable and a paddock opposite. Near the Angel Hill end of the street on the west side was the Independent Methodist Chapel, which had opened in 1828. Traders in the street included a broker (no qualification given), baker, clothier, blacksmith and plumber, and there was also a windmill, which is not drawn on the map, but was probably in what is now Fornham Road. Scurfe Lane, now that part of Cotton Lane which is at the back of the houses on the east side of the street and ends with Reeds Buildings, is described here. The rest of Cotton Lane came under the Mustow Street heading, which also included the Botanic Gardens and Abbey Grounds. In Mustow Street there were a coach-maker, brazier, farrier and grocer. Mustow House was then a school with its playground mentioned in its description. Over the bridge, Eastgate Street had a currier, a pastry shop, bakery, butcher, malt office and a wool warehouse, John Ridley's tannery in the Ancient House and a millwright's shop and yard. Tanning was carried on in this street in the 15th century, and the fire which destroyed much of the town centre in 1608 started in a malting here, so trades continued in the same streets, if not necessarily on the same sites.

The north end of Angel Hill already had a number of large houses. The then number 10 was described as a house, shop, bathrooms, yard and bake-office; in White's *Directory* of 1844 the occupier, John Botwright, was listed among the gentry and described as bathkeeper, the number by then being 12. There was a slaughter-house next to the Bull Inn while nearby, on part of the site where Crescent House is now, J.F.P. Harrington had a concert room. Almost every property on the north side of Abbeygate Street had a shop, and here as elsewhere in the town, most of the shopkeepers still lived in the same premises. There was a subscription Library which stood on part of the site where the Corn Exchange was built.

William Ray, a well-known local clockmaker, was one of the tradesmen who worked in Brentgovel Street. A dyer, baker, butcher, two plumbers, a shoemaker, broker and grocer also traded here. The building trades were well represented, with both John Trevethan and William Steggles having premises there as well as a carpenter called Miller. Looms Lane only had six properties, in addition to the almshouses near the corner of Garland Street. The residents on the north side of Angel Hill seem to have acquired land in Looms Lane to provide rear entrances to their large houses. Well Street had a few workshops, but its most notable feature was John Frost's stables and riding school. It is clear from the map that the fine houses on the east side, sometimes called St John's Terrace, had not yet been built. High Baxter Street had a shop which boasted an ice house, in addition to a currier, pipe-maker, blacksmith, brushmaker and maltster. It is appropriate that the Health Centre stands where Blomfield's School used to be, for it was there that Charles James Blomfield, the reforming Bishop, first of Chester and then of London, was born. As well as his involvement in setting up the Ecclesiastical (now Church) Commissioners and his church-building schemes in London, he was a friend of Chadwick and introduced in the House of Lords some of the legislation which laid the foundations of modern standards of public health. The Baptist Church was in this street, and their old burial ground can still be seen at the back of the Borough Offices car park, but the new chapel in Garland Street, built in 1834, is marked on Payne's map. Samuel Ridley had a foundry here and Thomas Ridley his chandler's office. Hunter's auction room was also in this street. The last street Payne surveyed in St James's parish was Garland Street, where the Methodists then had a chapel. This was a mainly residential street, apart from a shop and a hat manufactory, while in School Hall Lane there was a bakery.

Payne began his survey of St Mary's parish in Abbeygate Street, where every property but one included a shop. Mrs Stocking, at the then number 58, had the only wholly residential property. Thomas Ridley was already established with a draper's shop at 34 and a grocer's shop at 35. On Angel Hill, there were the Subscription Rooms, not yet the Athenaeum, as well as a printer and a bakery. J.G. Lenny, another early 19th century surveyor, had the house which used to stand between the

Cathedral and the Norman Tower. Athenaeum Lane appears as Pig Lane, not under its old name of Punch Lane. It became Athenaeum Lane after 1854.

Much of the property in Sparhawk Street belonged to Thomas De Carle, who was described in the 1844 *Directory* as a coach builder; it seems from Payne's account that at this date he also ran a waggon office from somewhere in the street. Apart from that the only business premises mentioned specifically was a bake-office. In St Mary's Square the Methodist Meeting House (now number 4A) was described as belonging to the Calvinists. There were ten houses in the Square, of which five belonged to owner-occupiers, a high proportion indeed for this date, and most had large gardens. Timothy Richard Holmes's house (with grounds of over four acres) is now the residential part of St Edmund's Nursing Home. Generally speaking, the houses in Raingate Street were small and under the heading 'Back of Raingate Street' there were a number of gardens containing anything between eight perches and an acre, as well as Nomans Meadows and Haberdon.

There were already many courts and yards off Southgate Street by 1833; between the corner of Prussia Lane and number 7 there were Lion Court, Badger Court and an unnamed yard, as well as the Almshouses in Long Row, which were built at right angles to the street in the manner of many of the courts, although the site there allowed for a spacious garden. However, some of the houses in the street were large with extensive grounds. In Out Southgate (Sicklesmere Road) there was the County Gaol and Bridewell. Commercial activities included two tanneries, one of which was run by the Ridley family and seems to have had Linnet House as its headquarters, a slaughter-house, three maltings, three bakeries, three windmills, a brick kiln in Out Southgate, a wheelwright's shop, cooper's shop and bullock sheds. A steelyard is mentioned in the description of Henry Rackham's property just north of the White Hart and, somewhere near the site of Alicia Court, James Young had a military storehouse. Maynewater Lane had only four houses, one of which had a bakery. At what stage, one wonders, did the medieval Mayde Water become Maynewater Lane?

The Theatre Royal and St Edmund's Roman Catholic church were the two public buildings in Westgate Street, but it must be remembered that the present Roman Catholic church building only dates from 1837. Immediately after the Theatre, Payne described four properties belonging to Benjamin Greene, including his brewery. Houses varied from humble to large, one of the latter being that of Frances Belgrave, at the then number 71, which had grounds of over an acre with an ice house. Out Westgate was included with Westgate Street and what is now Hospital Road, where the Suffolk General Hospital was then on a site of little more than an acre. Near the Hospital was an infants' school, perhaps that next to St Peter's church. In Vinery Lane, at Stamford Bridge Barns and on adjacent property, John Trevethan had, in addition to his brick kiln, two hot houses and a melon ground. The broker's and smith's shops mentioned were all in the outlying areas away from Westgate Street itself. There were three houses in Friars Lane.

St Andrews Street South was a mixture of mainly quite humble dwellings and a variety of commercial activity. Pump Court, which had fourteen houses, had been built by James Oakes in the 18th century to provide homes for those who worked in his combing shops; nearby, behind his Guildhall Street home, was Cobb's Orchard from which James Oakes had his crop of hay each year, a valuable commodity in the days of horse-drawn transport. Near Westgate Street there was a limekiln, while elsewhere two residents had bullock sheds, one in conjunction with a slaughter-house, and one a cow house. The next area to be surveyed was the north side of Field Lane. The National School, which is marked on Lenny's map nearly opposite Prospect Row, which is there called St Edmunds Place, is recorded just before Payne described Turkey Court, which later became part of the Boby Site. Two windmills, both depicted on the map, stood on this side of the street, one of them in what is now called Mill Road.

Guildhall Street, with Hog Lane connecting it to Whiting Street, was largely residential with a fairly high number of shops. There was still one butcher's shop in the street, and a slaughter-house, while there was a pawnbroker's shop in Hog Lane. Whiting Street, too, was largely residential. The Independent Meeting House is now the United Reformed Church. The proprietors of the short-lived *Bury Press* had their office at the north end of the west side of the street. Other trades included two bakeries, two curriers, a cooper and a butcher. Off Whiting Street was Elephant Court, with a school room and a residence for the school mistress. In Hatter Street Gedge and Barker, proprietors of the *Bury and Norwich Post,* founded in 1782, had their printing office at the Abbeygate Street end on the east side of the street, while Gedge and Son had an engine house and printing office almost opposite. There were seven unspecified shops as well as a butcher's and a baker's. Across Churchgate Street, houses in College Street tended on the whole to be more humble than those in Hatter Street, and there were two unnamed yards here as well as Zebra Court. The Lancastrian School was in this street and two blocks of almshouses, both of which have been converted into private houses; the former William Barnaby almshouses now front William Barnaby Yard, a group of town houses, and the former Holofernes Allen almshouses stood nearby on the other corner of Church Walks. Church Walks already had 31 houses, with five more in Weazel Court, which opened off it.

Bridewell Lane mainly consisted of modest dwellings, often gathered round a shared yard, with only a small proportion of the houses having any garden. There were three unnamed courts containing eleven, ten and five houses respectively. More rural in aspect was the paddock, with stables which Roger Boldero rented from the Guildhall Feoffees, and John Watson had an orchard and stable. It must have been crowded and Samuel Bett's slaughter-house and pigsties can have done little to improve the environment. There was only one substantial house in the street. Angel Lane had a number of houses, but also many stables, including those of the Angel, which extended through from Angel Hill. A. & J. Frost kept livery stables there and the Dog Tap-house also had stables. Churchgate Street reveals an unremarkable mix of properties, many houses having shops. The Unitarian chapel, built by the Presbyterians in 1711 was, and is, the most remarkable building in the street. The Regency-style houses on the south side of Chequer Square were not yet built and at this date number 1 Chequer Square was a shop. Payne's description of Crown Street began with the Post Office, which was then next to the Norman Tower. There was an infants' school with a house for the master in this street, and dyeing was carried out at two premises there. The name Honey Hill was used only for that part of the street which was west of Sparhawk Street on the south side of the street, but included the properties down to the entrance into the Churchyard on the opposite side of the road. The Manor House and houses around it were then regarded as part of School Hall Street, which continued round the corner into what is now part of Raingate Street.

This detailed survey of the town, with a keyed map of the land in the town and the printed map showing the buildings, which Payne published in 1834, provides an excellent basis for a study of the new streets and estates which began to appear as the town continued to grow. It should eventually be possible to see whether there were already factory-based industries, such as Dr Fiske identified in the case of James Oakes's combing shops in the 18th century, while the early directories should make it possible to identify specialist shops.

ABOVE: Out Risbygate developed as increased population caused houses to be built further from the town centre along existing roads. After the Barracks was built in 1878, it became the custom for people to follow the band back after Sunday morning church parades. (JAW) OPPOSITE: Lenny's map. RIGHT: By the beginning of the 19th century the need was felt for a third Anglican church. St John's, consecrated in 1842, has a spire which has become a major landmark; before 1910. (JAW)

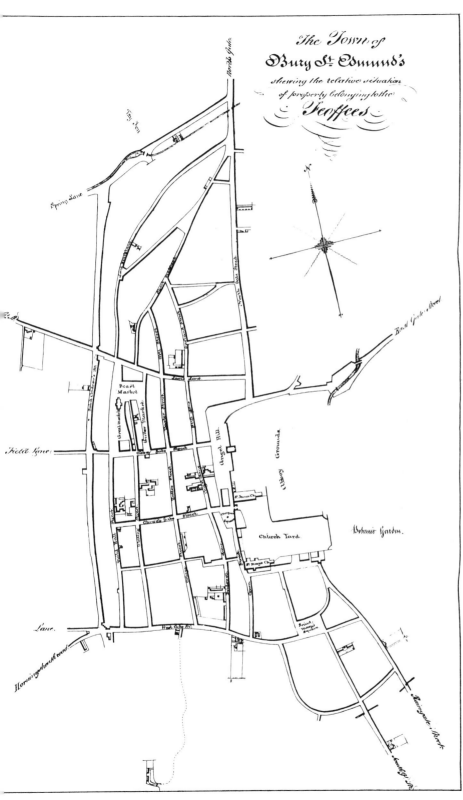

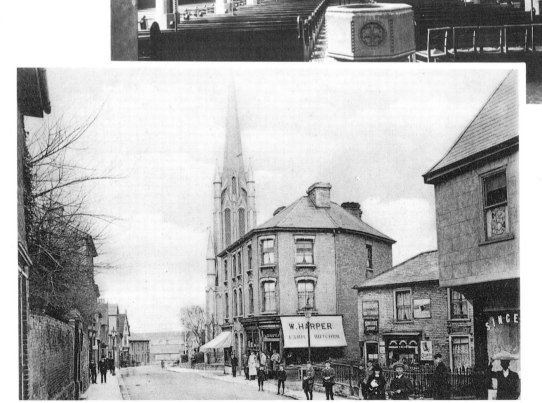

OPPOSITE ABOVE: Another view of Out Risbygate, before 1915, showing the Falcon Inn. (JAW) CENTRE: The interior of St John's Church early this century. (JAW) BELOW: After the opening of the Railway, St John's Street became an important route to the town centre. This card, from the early years of this century, shows the Singer Sewing Machine shop, a general store, with a front garden, and Harper's the Butchers. (JAW)

ABOVE: A Primitive Methodist Chapel was first opened on this site in Northgate Street in 1828. The building has been used for a variety of secular purposes in recent years; c1905. (JAW) BELOW: The Baptists' first chapel was in Lower Baxter Street, where their burial ground can still be seen. In 1834, a new chapel was built by the Steggles, though it is by no means clear whether they designed as well as built it; c1905. (JAW)

LEFT: The Congregational, now United Reformed Church, in Whiting Street, refronted in 1866; c1905. (JAW) RIGHT: Unsocial hours worked by railwaymen resulted in the Railway Mission, begun in a room in the Station Master's house in 1895. Numbers increased and the chapel, just beyond the railway bridge, was bult in 1900; before 1912. (JAW) BELOW: The Suffolk General Hospital was founded in 1825 in rural surroundings — Payne described it in 1833 under the Out Westgate heading. This photograph shows it as it was before 1908. (JAW)

50

ABOVE: In 1908, Mr Washington Charters, of Horringer Manor, volunteered to provide the balconies shown here; c1910. CENTRE: Houses in Hospital Road, pictured before 1915. (JAW) BELOW: The junction of Hospital Road and Out Westgate, before 1911. (JAW)

ABOVE: The coming of the railway encouraged building to fill in space in Northgate Street, seen here through the railway bridge before 1920. (JAW) BELOW: Looking through the railway bridge into Fornham Road, before 1905. (JAW)

ABOVE: The Wesleyan Middle-Class Boys' School began in Northgate Street but in 1885 Highland House, on Thomas Norfolk's Northgate Estate, was bought and extended to fit it for use as a School, later known as the East Anglian School. (First the boys, and more recently the girls, who took over these premises, have moved out to Culford.) The proximity of the railway station was much emphasised in Norfolk's publicity material. There used to be a stone near the end of Norfolk Road which read 'Norfolk Road (half a mile long) made and planted 1878'; c1925. (JAW) BELOW: Eastgate Street was also extended away from the town centre and part of it was, for a time, called Out Eastgate; before 1907. (JAW)

ABOVE: Deeds of the Cattle Market site show that houses were being built in Field Road, now Kings Road, early in the 19th century. Here a military and firefighters' cortège passes Salem Place on the way to the Cemetery. LEFT: Marie Louise de la Ramée, better known as the novelist Ouida, was born in 1839 in a house (marked with a plaque) in Union Terrace, Hospital Road. A great dog-lover during her lifetime, after her death in 1908 readers of the Daily Mirror subscribed for this memorial drinking fountain, which stands near the corner of Out Westgate and Vinery Road, an undeveloped country lane when this photograph was taken, before 1915. (MS) RIGHT: By the middle of the 19th century, the Great Church Yard was full and land was bought on the outskirts of the town, as it then was, for a cemetery, which opened in 1855. Two chapels were built, one for Anglicans and the other for dissenters, but only one remains now. They were designed by Mr Peck of Cooper and Peck, 1 Furnivals Inn, London. (MS)

LEFT: Another view of the Ouida Memorial shows old cottages at the bottom of Petticoat Lane, c1910; (MS) and RIGHT: looking towards the town, and the hill beside Petticoat Lane before it was developed, c1935. (JAW) CENTRE: Horringer Road, as it was at the beginning of this century. (JAW) BELOW: Springfield Road, before 1909. (JAW)

ABOVE: York Road in the first decade of this century. (JAW)
BELOW: These houses on the east side of Well Street are some of the
most attractive early Victorian infilling in the town. (MS)

ABOVE: Church Walks which, with Hog Lane, is a footpath from Crown Street to Guildhall Street, was already heavily built-up when Payne surveyed the town in 1833. These could be those which Steggles owned there. (MS) BELOW: This cottage in Home Farm Lane, which won a West Suffolk Architectural Award in 1973, was Swiss Cottage, at Hardwick, mentioned in the 1861 Census. (MS)

ABOVE LEFT: St John's Place is found in the 1861 Census. (MS)
RIGHT: Parts of Blomfield Street had been built before 1881. The
spire of St John's Church can be seen above the roof tops. (MS)
BELOW LEFT: Beaconsfield Terrace in Chalk Road was built in
1878. (MS) RIGHT: West View Cottages, in West Road, are dated
1884. They were on the limits of the town at the time and, when first
built, must have commanded good views. (MS)

ABOVE: When first built, Queens Road was called Upper Brown Road but, at the Town Council meeting of 3 May 1887, it was agreed that, from 21 June following, it should be called Queen's Road, to mark Queen Victoria's Golden Jubilee. This house, now the Post Office, was built that year. (MS)
BELOW: Two houses in Albert Crescent were under construction when the 1881 Census was taken. Albion Villas date from 1897. (MS)

ABOVE: Streets such as this were not built all at once. One house dated 1881 is next to another dated 1931. (MS) BELOW: The Priors Inn, opened 8 November 1933, by which date there was great pressure on building land to the west of the town. (MS)

THE MOVING MARKET

Before 1066 the town had its market, for a place which was the administrative centre of the western part of Suffolk, and had been given the right to have a mint, would have been commercially active and a marketing centre for the surrounding countryside.

It is the generally accepted view that the pre-Conquest market place was in St Mary's Square, which appears in 14th century and later documents as the Horse Market, otherwise the eld or old market. The present market place, in Cornhill and Buttermarket is said to have been laid out by Abbot Baldwin between 1066 and 1086. Angel Hill, which looks as though it was designed to be used as a market place, was used as the site of Bury Fair by the end of the medieval period, and this may well have been the case since the twelfth century. It was, as well as the great market, conveyed to the Alderman and Burgesses in 1608 as part of the land and soil on which the markets and fairs of the town had customarily been held. The present market area is easily recognisable in the 1295 tax assessment, but it may only recently have become a market area since, when the townsmen attempted to extort a charter from the Abbot during the revolt of 1327, one of their demands was that the markets should be returned to their ancient places. In bringing together information about the markets and fairs, and the places in which they were held, it seems clear that the accepted view is an over-simplification of a complex subject.

Much of our early information about the market, the fair and the market place comes from the time of Abbot Samson, 1182-1211. Jocelin of Brakelond tells us how the market was originally held on Sunday and the market day was changed to Tuesday after Eustace, the Prior of Saint-Gemer-de-Flay, had visited Bury St Edmunds in 1201 and preached against Sunday trading. The present market days, Wednesday and Saturday, with sometimes a cattle market on Monday, were fixed by the fifteenth century. We also know from Jocelin that there had been much encroachment on to the market place. In 1201, after the monks of Ely had attempted to start a market at Lakenheath, the Abbey acquired a charter from King John which enabled them to have competing markets, (which reduced the trade at Bury) suppressed. The results are clearly to be seen in a map showing medieval markets in Suffolk, where there are few in the immediate vicinity of Bury St Edmunds, and some of those are known to have been short-lived, quickly suppressed by the monks of St Edmund.

Following the accepted view that Baldwin laid out the present market place between 1066 and 1086, Jocelin's picture of the market can be set against its familiar background. Moyses Hall could be one of the stone houses built in the market place, and the Traverse, Skinner Street and the west side of Butter Market could be identified with the encroachments on the market about which the monks of Jocelin's time complained because, having developed into permanent shops, they were reducing the Abbey's income from tolls for market stalls. However, a clause in the extorted charter of 1327, which sought to restore the markets to their ancient places, compels us to reconsider this view.

While a market requires space for stalls erected on a few days each week, a major medieval fair would have required much more space, even though it was only held during a few weeks of the year. Angel Hill was the site of the Bury Fair by the end of the medieval period and it may have been its home from the time the right to hold a fair was granted to Abbot Anselm in the 1120s. It has been argued that Anselm enlarged the precinct westwards, to contain the parish churches and other buildings displaced by his enlarged plans for the Abbey church. It is known that he was responsible for building the precinct wall and gates. Anselm not only had the right to hold a market confirmed but, as he also acquired the right to hold a fair, he may well have had a keen eye to the commercial potential of Bury St Edmunds. It was during Anselm's abbacy that the men of Bury were granted freedom from toll throughout the realm, an important trading concession and, although we do not know the date when the guild merchant was established in the town, some date during Anselm's rule is most likely. Certainly, as merchants began to come to Bury from far and wide to trade at its fair, Bury merchants would wish to trade at other fairs of similar status and, without the communal regulation afforded by the guild merchant, this would scarcely have been feasible.

A short length of Northgate Street, from Pump Lane to Angel Hill, long retained High Street as an alternative name. It seems possible that Anselm might have built over what had been the town's main shopping street as he enlarged the precinct. Angel Hill, known until the seventeenth century as Mustowe, with its connotations of a meeting place for the inhabitants, would have made a splendid market place, strategically placed for a careful abbot and his officers to have kept an eye on its conduct, with a view to maximising their income.

From its beginnings in Anselm's time, Bury fair grew in prestige and became established as one of the major international trading fairs of medieval England. Anselm's grant was for a fair on St James's day, 25 July, and the days before and after but, during the time that Bury St Edmunds was among the more important trading fairs, it was between St Edmund's eve (19 November) and Christmas Eve that the town filled up with merchants. Walter of Pinchbeck, who tabulated the Abbey's rights after the revolt of 1327, also listed fairs held on the vigil of St Peter, 28 June, and the following day, and that which became the Bury Fair of later centuries, held on St Matthew's eve, 20 September, and the following day. No doubt, as in the eighteenth century, many temporary structures were thrown up each year to provide accommodation. Residents suffered considerable disruption, as owners of properties in the market place, wherever it might have been, were required to give up their shops to whomsoever the Sacrist or other owner might require. This is shown, for example, in a deed dating from 1182-1186, which related to property in the market, made between the Sacrist and Serlo the tanner. During the feast of St Edmund, the Sacrist was free to let the ground floor of the house next to the street and the square to merchants coming to the town for St Edmund's fair. This was a standard procedure in towns which acted as hosts to major international fairs. Did Samson and his Sacrist hold the market and fair on Angel Hill or in the Great Market — or both?

Ellen Wedemeyer Moore has gathered together a great deal of information about the more important fairs of medieval England which, insofar as the evidence has survived, gives a glimpse of the business transacted. She stresses the importance of good communications in the siting of these fairs. Places relatively close to Bury St Edmunds, such as Mildenhall and Brandon, were thriving ports in the middle ages and it is possible that the Lark was used to carry goods even closer to the town. Whatever the state of medieval roads, Bury St Edmunds is shown on the 14th century Gough map on the only 'main' road through East Anglia, branching off from Cambridge through Bury to Norwich. The east of England was the home of the early centres of cloth production, and there was a thriving cloth-making industry in Bury itself, so local clothmakers found the fair an excellent mart for their wares. To give some idea of the distances involved Ms Moore gives details of transactions made by merchants from Lincoln, Beverley and Stamford as well as foreign traders from Douai, Ypres and Poperinghe. Goods bought and sold included canvas, cloth (which could have been either silk or wool) from Arras, cloth of gold, cords, hair cloths, cushions, napkins and towels, silk and tapets. Among purchases made for the Royal household at Bury St Edmunds were horses and furs. A Lincoln merchant, Stephen of Stanham, who is known to have traded here in 1303, at various times in the course of his career is known to have dealt in cloth, wax, sugar, fish, nuts, ginger, rice and miniver hoods. Ms Moore is surely right to emphasise that the host community for these vast trading events must have been populous and that careful organisation would have been necessary to arrange such essentials as accommodation for the traders and the security of their wares. There seems to be no evidence which throws light on such arrangements in Bury St Edmunds, but it is possible that the names of some of the areas relating to trading activities could well have been those allotted to merchants visiting for the fair, rather than residents who traded all the year round. Goldsmiths' and Glovers' Row, which extended from the Abbey Gate to the Norman Tower, could have been one such area, for it is unlikely that there were enough indigenous goldsmiths and glovers, producing costly luxury items, who would have required such an area during that early period. Similarly, Frenchmen's Street, which seems to have been a name once used for the east end of Abbeygate Street, is just as likely to have been so called because the French merchants were provided with lodging there during the fair, as being named from the French craftsmen who were encouraged to settle in the town by Abbot Baldwin. Disputes between merchants at the fair frequently seem to have been heard at a court held in the Churchyard rather than in the regular town court held in the Toll House, which may be a further indication that Angel Hill was always used for the fair.

The importance of St Edmund's fair seems to have declined in the fourteenth century. The revolts which troubled the town from time to time must have discouraged traders from coming to Bury St Edmunds, and the unfortunate co-incidence of St Edmund's feast, on 20 November, with poor weather, at a date when winter travel must have been uncomfortable and hazardous in the extreme, would also deter all but the most intrepid. But, as a local mart for trading in cloth, it continued for centuries to have its place in the economic life of the town, while early in the 19th century citizens still purchased their winter provisions at the fair. It had, of course, long combined trade with entertainment, and was essentially a fun fair when it was discontinued in 1871.

Because the monks were so alarmed at the failure of their income from the market to rise as it had done in most other towns, one of the remedies they suggested, as reported by Jocelin of Brakelond, was that the market should be moved to another site. Samson would not agree to this, but Jocelin implied that the monks hoped that in future, under a more amenable abbot than Samson, they might be able to move the market to another site. This must have happened at some time in the 13th century, and it was then that the market was moved into the Cornhill/Buttermarket area. According to the *Bury Chronicle*, a serious fire in 1215 destroyed a third of the town. This could have provided a favourable moment for adjustments to the town plan; it could even have cleared a space for a new market place. Early references to the market give no clues to its location, though the 1295 tax assessment shows that the Great Market was clearly settled in the Butter Market/Cornhill area by then.

In the light of the clause in the extorted charter of 1327, it is difficult to believe that the Cornhill/Buttermarket market place was laid out between 1066 and 1086. It seems impossible that the townsmen could still have resented a change made more than two hundred years before.

One of Abbot Samson's deeds shows him selling off a large building plot, at Paddock Pool, the area near Chequer Square and the Athenaeum. In the 16th century the site where the Athenaeum now stands was known as *les Rowes*, a name redolent of marketing activity. The plot was 90 feet long by 53 feet wide whereas, to give some idea of relative sizes, the Athenaeum ballroom is 73 feet long by 37 feet wide. The identification of the two sites must not be pressed too hard, but it would do no harm to keep this possibility in mind for, in the earliest of the Athenaeum deeds, dated 1713, Punch Lane was still given Paddock Pool as its alternative.

But this is not to say that the Butter Market/Cornhill market place was, in modern planning terms, a green field site, for Moyses Hall stands to this day to remind us that something happened in that part of the town in the last years of the 12th century. From 1182-1200 there is a deed relating to property *in magna platea versus aquilonem in villa sancti Ædmundi*, that is in the great square towards the north. Could this refer to an open place, west of the Abbey, but in the northern part of the town?

Despite the changes in street names, the present market place can be recognised in the 1295 tax assessment. But Linendraper Row, which was well developed before 1433, is somewhat troublesome. The Sacrist had nine properties there in both 1433 and 1526, and more buildings are indicated in the abuttals. It has been suggested that a tiny space between the properties on the west side of Butter Market and those on the east side of Skinner Street could represent the site of Linendraper Row. Aerial photographs of the market area show that, although a number of shops now extend through from Butter Market to Skinner Street, this is not so in every case, and the small gap between the two rows of buildings can still be seen in places; it was already in part built over when Payne made his map of the town in 1833. Recent investigations of buildings in the Traverse, which now include those formerly on the west side of Skinner Street at the back, show that there were fine buildings in medieval Skinner Street, which could merit a site in a more spacious street than the present one. It is possible that the market was re-organised after the fire of 1608, as the block which now includes the east side of Skinner Street and the west side of Butter Market dates from after the fire.

One change which took place in the market area after the dissolution is well documented. Ratten, Rawton or Rotten Row, which extended south from a property on the site where Dorothy Perkin's shop is now, as far south as the site of the Market Cross, was one of many parts of the market place which was extensively damaged, if not utterly destroyed, in the fire of April 1608. Deeds remaining among the archive of the Guildhall Feoffees show that the Feoffees bought up the sites where these buildings had stood and they have never been rebuilt. Even in 17th century terms, they must have been impeding the flow of traffic about the market place.

To what extent the use of street or row indicated the original width of the street requires some investigation. The ancient legislation which required a street to be sufficiently wide to allow either two laden carts to pass, or sixteen armed soldiers to march side by side, may well have been more honoured in the breach than the observance. Suffice it to point out that rows are found in Bury only in what are now the Angel Hill and Cornhill/Butter Market area, and in Abbeygate Street which joins these areas. Much of this area, by 1295, was in what was often called, as an alternative to the Risbygate Ward, the High Ward. If High is used in this instance in the same sense as in High Street, which is usually used for the main trading street of a town, this might indicate a ward largely devoted to the town's mercantile activities.

Attempts were being made to move the Fishmarket, which during the medieval period was at the Abbeygate Street end of the market place, when the town was petitioning for a charter early in the 17th century. A lease of a fish stall dated 8 August 1606, just after the incorporation of the borough but before the Corporation had been granted the reversion of the fairs and markets, has survived, but gives no indication of its location. This stall, which was let to a John Tomson of Elmswell, cardmaker, was built of freestone and was six feet nine inches in length and 3 feet nine inches wide. One (the east) end abutted on a fish stall used by William Cage, and the west end on another, rarely used, stall, made with timber and planks. The rent was 6s 8d a year, the tenant responsible for repairs. Warren, in 1747, placed the butter and fish markets in the area now called the Butter Market.

The Toll House, on the west side of Cornhill, had long been the building in which the Sacrist held his courts and in which deeds were often witnessed by the Alderman and Bailiffs of the town. It was one of those buildings which were damaged in the 1608 fire and was afterwards granted to the Corporation, who were left to rebuild or repair it to make it fit for use again. On the incorporation of the Borough, the courts were moved to the Guildhall and a lease of 1610 indicates that by then the Toll House had been repaired and extended to convert it into the Market House or Market Hall, later known as the Wool Hall, which has given its name to Woolhall Street. It was to this building that merchants brought the considerable quantities of wool sold in the markets in Bury until the 19th century.

Scharff's superb watercolour, which may be seen at the Record Office, shows the spaciousness of the market before the two 19th century corn exchange buildings, one of which is now converted into shops, were built. Payne's survey shows that virtually every building around the market place included a shop or a warehouse. Oakes and Bevan's Bank is recorded, and it may be worth mentioning that T. C. Billingham had a laboratory as well as his shop in the building immediately north of the Suffolk Hotel.

By the end of the 18th century the market was growing out of the Cornhill/Butter Market area and the Cattle Market was moved, not without opposition, to a new site in St Andrews Street South in 1828, which had formerly formed part of Spintlemill Field, one of the old open fields of the town. Plans are now being discussed in which the removal of the Cattle Market is once again proposed, a suggestion which does not find universal favour. There is little chance of moving a market place in Bury without stirring up public feeling.

ABOVE: Sketch plan to show how part of Northgate Street could be what was left of the town's main street prior to enlargement of the precinct. A Length of Northgate Street from Pump Lane to Angel which had High Street as an alternative name; B Supposed line of continuation of this street across the precinct as enlarged; C Mustowe, indicating a meeting place, which may well have been planned as a market place and/or fairground.
BELOW: Cornhill before 1905: the Market Cross is shown before alterations to its roof when it was repaired after the fire in 1908. Part of the Post Office is on the extreme right of the picture. The building next to it was replaced by Boots' old premises, now John Menzies, while the Three Kings Inn was replaced by Burton's shop. (JAW)

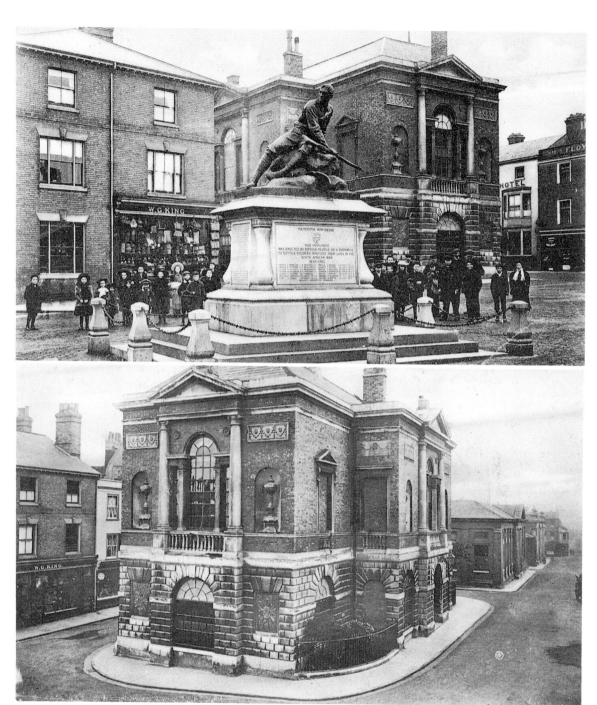

ABOVE: This Memorial to the Suffolk Soldiers who lost their lives in the South African War, 1899-1902, was unveiled by Lord Methuen on 11 November 1904. Also in the picture was W. G. King's brushmakers' shop, part of the Three Kings, and the adjoining shop, then Floyds County Drug Store; before 1908. (JAW) BELOW: The Market Cross, then the Town Hall, before 1908. Beyond it is the School of Art now, after a variety of other uses, converted into shops, and the Corn Exchange. (JAW)

*ABOVE: A lively Market Day scene before 1907. (MS) BELOW:
Another view of Cornhill, between 1903 and 1912. (MS)*

ABOVE: This view of a busy market day dates from c1920. Little of the west of Cornhill, seen in the background, has survived 1960s rebuilding. (JAW) BELOW: Cornhill, with Moyses Hall, and, beyond it, The Castle, Smith's furniture store and Lawsons. Late 1930s. (MS)

LEFT: The 'bus in this photograph of Cornhill gives its destination as Rougham Flower Show; c1935. (JAW) RIGHT: The Traverse, before 1939, when the Drinking Fountain was moved to the Abbey Gardens. (JAW) BELOW: Cornhill and Buttermarket c1955; the 'bus station can be seen between Moyses Hall and Palmer's Restaurant. The Milk Bar and Bata Shoes are in the premises which are now Dixon's. (MS)

ABOVE: In July 1906, as a fund-raising venture, the Aldeburgh life boat and its crew visited Bury St Edmunds. Some of the cavalcade of decorated vehicles are seen here in Butter Market. (JAW) BELOW: Large open spaces are always at risk from the motor car. This photograph of Angel Hill was taken in the 1930s, and shows that it was already taking on the character of a car park. (JAW)

LEFT: *Joseph Clarendon Smith's painting of the St Matthew's Fair is signed and dated 1808. In addition to all the animation of the fair, Smith depicts buildings around Angel Hill, leaving out the cupola on the top of the Norman Tower, which was only removed in 1845. (St Eds) RIGHT: Cattle Market, St Andrew's Street South before 1906; the area in the foregound is now a car park, but the settling house still stands, although in a dilapidated state. When it was put up in 1864, the Toll Collector was given permission to sell ginger beer and buns from it on market days. (JAW) BELOW: The settling house on the St Andrews Street South Cattle Market is a most attractive building — David Gentleman included a sketch of it in his book Gentleman's Britain. It is now very dilapidated and boarded up; one hopes that its future is secure.*

*The Norman Tower as it was before the Cupola was removed in the
course of its restoration in 1845 from Yates, Antiquities. (MS)*

BEHIND THE WALLS

Those who lived in medieval Bury would have been familiar with the magnificence of the buildings which stood behind the precinct wall. In the early days, until a *modus vivendi* between Abbey and town made it unnecessary, they would have been in the habit of entering the precinct by one of its gates to go to church. The 13th century *Liber Albus* mentions that Ralph, Bishop of Rochester, 1108-1114, held a confirmation in the monk's cemetery, about where St Andrew's chapel was later built. Traders — especially merchants in town for Bury Fair — who had to take action for debt and such like claims, usually preferred to have their cases heard in the Abbot's court, which sat in the Churchyard, rather than in the town court at the Toll House. Jocelin of Brakelond wrote of Boxing Day entertainment in the churchyard in the last years of the twelfth century. If the historian Gillingwater is correct — and, unfortunately, this is not always the case — in the 15th century the Fair spilt over from Angel Hill into the walks in the Abbey court. Candlemas guild said prayers in the Charnel chapel. And, at last, the townspeople would be buried within the precinct walls. Everyone knew what there was behind those high walls.

The walls round the precinct were built during the time of Abbot Anselm, 1121-1148, and there were only four gates. On the south side, there was St Margaret's Gate, where the road now goes into the Churchyard. The two main entrances (both still standing) were on the west side; the Cemetery or St James's Gate, which is now known as the Norman Tower, and the Court Gate which is now called the Abbey Gate. The fourth entrance was from Mustow Street. On the west and north sides of the precinct a drainage ditch ran, moat-like, before the walls, and access to the gates was over wooden bridges. During Anselm's time, 1121-1148, both parish churches had been built within the precinct walls and, as long as the town was liable to revolt against its monastic masters, the entrances to the parish churches must have been from within the precinct. When St Mary's church tower was built in about the year 1400, it was kept within the precinct wall, but when the nave and aisles were enlarged between 1424 and c1433 they extended outside the precinct wall at the west end. This may well be the explanation of the mystery which surrounds John Nottyngham's bequest for building porches on the south and west sides of the church. When he made his will in 1437 these two doors would have been new features of the church, and the abbot's permission would be needed to build porches before them, extending the church even further into the street. It may well have been that the abbot's permission was not forthcoming. For whatever reason, Nottyngham's executors built — or, more likely — up-dated, a porch on the north side, where it protects a 14th century doorway, which would, until then, have been the main entrance into the church.

St James's Church was similarly entered from the Churchyard until the sixteenth century. In the summer of 1503, work began to extend St James's Church to the street and it can be shown from rentals relating to property belonging to the Sacrist of St Edmunds that this involved the demolition of at least three shops, which had formerly stood on the site where the west end of the nave was built. There are many references in medieval wills to the porch of St James's church, which also served as a chapel dedicated to the Virgin Mary. As the main entrance to St Mary's had been on the north side of that church, the porch of St James's Church, mentioned in 15th century wills, must have been on the south side.

By the time of the dissolution, there may have been a number of other places where the precinct wall had been breached. In about 1529 the Abbot, Prior and Convent granted a 99 year lease, at an annual rent of 6s 8d, to George Watton, mercer, of a house and orchard belonging to the office of the Sub-Sacrist, which was between the cemetery of the church of St James on the east and the stone wall of the cemetery on the west. It abutted on the tower of St James' church (the Norman Tower) to the north, and a curtilage let to William Holyour, clerk, south, and was 105 feet from north to south and 23 feet from east to west, next to the tower, and 18 feet at its southern end. The description of the property mentioned that a stream of water ran through the walls in the cemetery. This watercourse may be connected with the drainage ditch which used to run around the precinct wall from Crown Street to Eastgate Bridge. The area near the Norman Tower is low-lying and was known as Paddock Pool. Storm water from Churchgate Street and Crown Street would have collected by the base of the tower and a subsidiary drain, perhaps culverted, to cope with excess storm water from Churchgate Street and Crown Street, could well have been required if the drainage ditch round the precinct wall was unable to cope with a sharp storm. In addition to showing that there was at least one house and a curtilage within the precincts, the covenants make it clear that George Watton, the lessee, already had a gate through the precinct wall next to the Norman Tower and he was given permission to make another to give direct access into his orchard. The survival of one stray lease such as this indicates that leases may have been made of other parts of the precinct before the dissolution of the Abbey of St Edmund.

The available evidence about the fate of the Abbey site between 1539 and 1560 is scanty. On 28 May 1550 it was leased to an influential courtier, Sir Anthony Wingfield, a Suffolk man who rose to be Comptroller of the Household to Edward VI. He had been Sheriff of Norfolk and Suffolk in 1515-1516 and was Member of Parliament for Suffolk from 1529-1535 and became a Privy Councillor in the year Bury Abbey was dissolved. When John Eyer, the Receiver for the County of Suffolk, bought the site, he paid £412 19s 5d, which does not seem a great deal, even in 16th century terms, if it still had substantial remains of one of the greatest medieval churches in the country and extensive conventual buildings standing on it. He had paid half as much again for the houses and plots of land which had formerly belonged to the Abbey of St Edmund and Thetford Priory, and some other former monastic land in Suffolk, which he bought in 1540. Those who excavated the Abbey church in the 1950s and 1960s reported that the ashlar had been removed from the walls while they were still standing, from scaffolding. It is known that, when the shrine of Our Lady of Woolpit was demolished in 1551, those who carried out the work on behalf of the Crown were required, once they had removed the lead, to have the stone, timber and other materials of the shrine valued before, on behalf of the Crown, selling the materials for the best price that could be got. There must have been similar instructions about the disposal of the materials from Bury Abbey. When Sir Nicholas Bacon acquired the site of St Saviour's Hospital from the Crown, as we know from a letter he wrote to one of his sons, he promptly gave orders to cart useable building materials to Redgrave, where his new house was under construction. There is little mystery about what happened to the materials from Bury Abbey. Within easy carting distance of Bury St Edmunds, there are a large number of 16th century houses built with re-used stone, and earlier timber-framed houses in which the 16th century chimney stack is stone built. Stone salvaged from the Abbey was used. Good building stone is not found in this area; it has always been expensive and was normally used sparingly, except by wealthy persons or organisations. There must have been a regular business in architectural salvage carried on in the years immediately following the dissolution, and the result of this commercial activity survives in the farmhouses built with medieval stones in the villages around about the town.

Some of the lead remained on the roof of the abbey church until it was removed to fulfil a contract which had been made by Henry VIII to provide the Earl of Warwick, the High Admiral, with 3,000 fothers of lead, at £4 6s 8d the fother; (a fother originally denoted a cartload, and then, in the case of lead, came to mean a fixed weight equivalent to a cartload, being generally in modern times 19½ cwt). By 1551, in the reign of Edward VI, 750 fothers remained to be delivered to Acelyne Salvage, to whom the Earl had assigned some of the lead, in full satisfaction of the 3,000 fothers. To complete this transaction the Court of Augmentations issued a warrant for removing the lead from the body of the church and the north and south aisles. John Eyer's accounts for this work survive, and cover everything from payments to 'Watchmen for keeping the leade from stealinge' to the skilled plumber's work carried out by John Regate, Paule Butcher and Thomas Brand, who were responsible for 'the cuting, pullynge down, melting into sowes and weiynge of lxxxvij fotheres and xij Cwt. of leade after iijs. iiijd. for every fother', which came to £12 16s 8d, while the 'riding charges' of three men, and their three servants 'to and from Sainte Edmondes Bury and liying there giving attendaunce upon the same by the space of xxxiij ti. daies after ixs for themselfes three servauntes and vj horses for every day amounteth to in the hole xiiij li xvijs'. The whole operation cost £36 2s 2d. The warrant was dated 9 March 1551 and the work no doubt was carried out soon afterwards. Diarmaid MacCulloch has suggested that part of the Abbey church may have remained roofed for so long because of the delay in completing the rebuilding of the nave of St James's Church. The difficulty in fundraising, which seems to have delayed the start of the rebuilding of St James's and caused its slow progress, could have been the reason why part of the Abbey church remained roofed for so long after the dissolution, for the parishioners would have needed somewhere to hold their services.

When, subject to the existing lease to Wingfield, the Abbey site was sold to John Eyer in 1560, most of the saleable building materials would have gone. Eyer was already living in a house within the precinct for some time before 1560 when he bought the Abbey site, Nomans Meadow, the Vinefield and Haberdon, for £412 19s 4d. By and large there are few differences, other than one or two variations in the order in which the parts of the site are described, from the earlier Latin deeds and that of 1588. Eyer's grant makes it clear that the monastic water supply with its pipes and cisterns was still in working order and was to be kept so. The Crown reserved the right to all bells and lead, except for lead in windows, gutters and the water pipes, and advowsons and rights of patronage were also excepted. It surely cannot have been intended to convey the parish churches to Eyer; could the reference to bells simply mean that bells were still in some remaining tower or towers of the Abbey church? The mansion in which Eyer, and later Badby, lived was already in existence in 1560 but it was only in 1580 that the tower on the north part of the great court was first mentioned. This seems to indicate that a second residence, or at least a substantial additon to the house in which Eyer had lived, had been created within the precinct.

The house in which Eyer and Badby had lived continued as a dwelling house until it was pulled down by Major Richardson Pack in 1720. The site of the former Great Court of the Abbey was then acquired by the Davers family in 1727, from whom it passed by descent to the Marquis of Bristol upon the death of Miss Davers in 1805. A Botanic Garden was established there in 1831, which has gradually developed into the Abbey Gardens as we know them today.

When Celia Fiennes visited Bury St Edmunds in 1698 she was dismissive of most of the houses in Bury. The gentry houses, she wrote, were in a place called the Green, which was a space by the two churches. It seems probable that she had in mind the houses in and around the former precinct.

The deeds of the Abbey site do not include those properties whcih stood under the Abbey wall. Before the dissolution there were many buildings huddling there, mainly houses or shops, but also including the monastic song school, the hall of the Duze Guild in Honey Hill and some almshouses in Crown Street. The well-known print of the balloon ascent from Bury St Edmunds in 1785 shows a building of ecclesiastical appearance and medieval date, adjoining the north side of the Abbey Gate; when Joseph Clarendon Smith painted Bury Fair in 1808, he recorded nothing more than the line denoting where the roof had been, which can still be seen.

The almshouses in Crown Street, which stood where the ornamental cherries are now, were demolished in 1813. It is possible that some of the former song school buildings and the hall of the Duze Guild (whose first members were said to have been the secular priests who were ousted when the Benedictines arrived in Bury) may have been incorporated within the houses east of St Mary's Church in Honey Hill. One of these, formerly known as St Margaret's Gate, is to be rehabilitated by the Town Trust. In 1692, Abraham Wright was beautifying and adding to a building on this site, and obtained a faculty to enclose part of the Churchyard to afford a rear access. When Wright died in 1702 his house, almost certainly the one on the site of the house later called St Margaret's Gate, had a hall, dining room, parlour, closet, pantry, cellars, kitchen, brew house, two closets by the kitchen, a stair case, best chamber, dressing room, parlour chamber, closet, kitchen chamber, maid's chamber, first garret, long garret and a study, to name them in the order in which they were valued for probate, and the furnishings and ornaments were plentiful and luxurious. A codicil to his will mentioned his set of twelve pictures of Roman Emperors, which he was anxious should not be split up among members of the family. The house was modernised in the 19th century and many features of that period still remain.

When the Davers bought the Abbey site, after Major Richardson Pack had demolished the sixteenth century dwelling house within the Abbey court, they followed the practice of up-grading a house just outside the precinct wall, with which the Abbey grounds could be used as a garden. The Abbey House on Angel Hill remained their family home until Lord Bristol sold it in 1831. It remained a private house until 1862 when Miss Fulcher's school was established there. Despite use as a school, and more recently as flats, it retains some fine architectural features and it was carefully restored last year.

The Churchyard was soon separated from the mansion house and the site of the former great court of the Abbey. The deeds of the Churchyard no longer include the deed by which it was first separated from the rest of the abbey site. Edward Cope, who owned the site from 1594, or Erasmus Cope, to whom it had passed by 1602, seem the likeliest owners to have sold it away, and Thomas Peede seems to have been one, perhaps the first, of its early owners, and Francis Mountford the second. The earliest surviving deed is an arrangement between Mountford's heirs, the Skinners, from which it is clear that certain parts had already been enclosed and these were specifically excluded from the conveyance of the remainder of the Churchyard. The Chapel of the Charnel seems to have been restored to the whole in the Skinner's deed of 1619, for it was left to Francis Skinner individually and in his will Mountford said that he had bought it from William Paine.

The main entrance to the Churchyard was through the archway of the Norman Tower. No doubt there would have been a footway open to all, at least during daylight hours, but in 1730 the lessee of the Churchyard was charging those who lived in the south of the town a yearly sum, to allow them to bring their coaches in through St Margaret's Gate to save them driving round to the Norman Tower. This is made clear in the papers relating to a dispute about liability for repairing St Margaret's Gate, which then belonged to a Mrs Monk. She claimed it as heir-at-law to Frances, wife of Hamon L'Estrange, who had inherited the Black Lion, to which the gate was attached, in 1711. The Black Lion was the inn next to Shire Hall, later known as the Magpie. When Mrs L'Estrange and her sister, Mrs Monk, inherited the Black Lion and St Margaret's Gate in 1711, the gateway, with a solar, or chamber, over it, was in a poor state of repair and, had it not been repaired, would very likely have fallen down. Mr L'Estrange had paid for rebuilding the gate in 1711, and Mr Bircham, the owner of the Churchyard, was therefore endeavouring to make Mrs Monk responsible for subsequent repairs. The case sets out that while this work, paid for by Mr L'Estrange, was going on 'five or six Gentlemen Feoffees or Lords of the Waste ground of Bury aforesaid came to him and insisted on the said Gate to belong to them, and he ought not to meddle with any of the Materials thereof'. Mr L'Strange sought leave to take away the old gateway and was given leave to do so, provided that he put up a new gate in its place. This is presumably the gateway shown in the illustration. It is uncertain who the five or six gentlemen were, unless the Corporation counted the gates into the precinct as town gates, which seems unlikely. The inn, first called the Black Lion and then the Magpie, was demolished in 1871 and its site (now the car park at the west end of the old Shire Hall building) became part of the garden of the house then known as St Margaret's Gate. A tunnel under the road into the Churchyard linked the two parts of the garden.

79

Some of the areas within the Churchyard which had been enclosed by an early date can be identified and, in some cases, a little is known about their past. The houses known nowadays as 1 and 2 Abbey Precincts seem to be the property which was leased by William Hayward to Judith Mully, widow, on 15 October 1672. A coin of Charles II was found when the house was being divided into two in the 1960s, so it may be that the house was newly built in 1672. Before the dissolution, the Sacrist's house and offices stood in the area where this house is now, but it is doubtful whether any medieval fabric has been included within the present structure, although the Chapel of St Andrew is within the garden.

In many places around the Churchyard the precinct wall has been cut through or, in places, entirely removed. Robert Nunn, a well known 19th century musician, who was born at the house called St Margaret's, which adjoins and is now used as part of the Shire Hall complex, recorded in his memoirs that his parents had their drawing room wall — the precinct wall — cut through, with considerable difficulty, to enable them to build on a connecting music room (now the Registrar's Marriage Room) in 1826, the year of his birth. The origins of this house, on the site of the former St Margaret's chapel, are obscure, but it is possible that it may be the house 'in or near the Churchyard' in which Lady Ann Hervey was living when she made her will in 1771, and which appears to have been her home for a number of years before her death. It is not clear whether part of the structure of St Margaret's chapel had been converted for secular use immediately after the dissolution, or whether the house called St Margaret's was built much later. The old monastic grammar school had been converted into a Shire House for the county courts and Thomas Badby conveyed it to the Guildhall Feoffees in 1578.

The change from ecclesiastical to secular use is known to have been effected quite quickly in a number of instances. The Chapel of the Charnel was already a private house in 1614, when Francis Mountford left it to his godson, Francis Skinner. Another chapel which was converted to secular uses was the Chapel of St-John-at-Hill, just behind the precinct wall in Crown Street. In 1602 it belonged to Edward Cope, who had bought it from Sir Robert Jermyn and Henry Blagg in 1593. When he sold it to Thomas Howe for £4 in 1602, it was described as a garden and ground, enclosed with stone walls. Howe annexed it to property in Crown Street, and it remained in use as a garden until 1625, when the site was built on. In the following year the new house, or part of it, was called the Schoolhouse, with two chambers over, two garrets over the chambers, and one little yard on its north side. Although it was started as a private venture, on 12 November 1627 the governors of the Grammar School bought it and it served as the English School, a preparatory department for the Grammar School. There was a dispute about the right of way through the yards from Crown Street in 1711, and some account of it in the 18th century is given in *The Story of King Edward VI School*. In December 1762 the Governors decided that Thomas Harley, the Master of the Poor Boys School in the Churchyard, should be paid his salary of ten pounds a year to Christmas next and no longer. The layout of the English School is recorded in Warren's plan of 1747, and stone walls, doubtless many times repaired if not entirely renewed, enclosing the yard of number 6 Crown Street, still indicate the site of this monastic chapel.

When Celia Fiennes visited Bury St Edmunds in 1698 she would have seen a fair number of gentlemen's houses around the Churchyard. There was that of Abraham Wright in Honey Hill, and what is now called Abbey Precincts, which seems to have been built in the 1670s. The house which was later owned by Lady Ann Hervey may already have been built, and is likely to be that now called St Margaret's, east of Shire Hall. Whether the Charnel was quite in this high class league is not by any means certain, but some of the Crown Street houses, near the Norman Tower, may well have been fitting residences for gentlemen. Old photographs of the Magpie suggest if was a substantial building and was owned and, it seems, occupied by gentry in the first half of the eighteenth century. This is suggested by the account of the trial of Arundel Coke, who lived nearby in Honey Hill, and attempted to have his brother-in-law, Edward Crisp, murdered in 1723. Coke persuaded Crisp to walk into the Churchyard with him on the pretext of visiting the Mrs Monk who had to take legal advice about her liability for repairing St Margaret's Gate.

William Lee gave his opinion on Mrs Monk's case in 1730, the year in which Lord Oxford visited Bury St Edmunds and, among other things, noted in his journal that avenues of trees had been planted in the Churchyard. Warren's map of 1747 shows that these were the avenues from the Nottyngham porch to near the Norman Tower and from there, by the west side of the Charnel, to near the site of St Margaret's Gate. Lord Oxford does not say what trees were planted, but David Elisha Davy, in his collections for the history of Suffolk, quotes a passage which refers to avenues of poplars, although now, and ever since photographs have been taken, limes have been planted.

Apart from the churches, the most distinguished building in the Churchyard is the Provost's House, built as Clopton's Hospital, into which the first residents were admitted in 1744.

After being in private hands from 1560, the Churchyard was conveyed to the Bury St Edmunds Corporation in 1798 and it remains the property of St Edmundsbury Borough Council.

ABOVE LEFT: The Norman Tower after cleaning in 1991. (MS) RIGHT: The Abbeygate was also cleaned last year and many details have been revealed which had long been obscured by grime and dirt. It seems easier now to appreciate that the Abbey was a building of the first importance and, had it stood in anything like its entirety, Bury St Edmunds would have buildings of international importance. (MS) BELOW LEFT: This view of Samson's Tower and part of the Churchyard dates from the 1930s. The railings round the graves were removed during the War, and almost all the gravestones were cleared in 1958. Motorists had already discovered the potential of the Churchyard as a car park. (JAW) RIGHT: The blinds in this photograph emphasise the domestic nature of the West Front. When the photograph was taken in 1930s, people lived in all the houses built into it. (JAW)

ABOVE: The Abbey site was excavated by the Ministry of Works, now English Heritage, between 1957 and 1964. As can be seen from this photograph, the ruins were fenced off from the Abbey Gardens, and there was a fair amount of ivy growing on the stonework and brambles and other bushes grew among them. The ruins of the Queen's Hall are in the foreground and the Abbot's Bridge can be seen in the distance; c1935. (JAW) BELOW: The Abbey Gate, from Yates, Antiquities; the medieval building shown in the drawing of the balloon ascent has given place here to a shed-like structure. (MS)

ABOVE LEFT: The interior of the Abbey Gate, from Yates, Antiquities. (MS) RIGHT: The Dovecote is little changed since this photograph was taken in the 1930s. (JAW) BELOW LEFT: St Margaret's Gate, as rebuilt in the eighteenth century, from Yates, Antiquities. (MS) RIGHT: The east wall of Scott's chancel in St James's Church, decorated with mosaics which can be seen in this photogaph dating from before 1909. (JAW)

84

ABOVE: This picture of the West Front and Samson's Tower dates from the early 1860s, before the railings had been put round the graves and the area planted with shrubs. Broken gravestones were used as edging. (JAW) BELOW: St James's Church, showing Scott's chancel of 1865-1869; after the church became the Cathedral of the new diocese of St Edmundsbury and Ipswich, this was too small for Cathedral services, and was replaced by a new choir, designed by Stephen Dykes Bower and consecrated in 1970; c1905 (JAW)

LEFT: Before the porch was built in 1961, the font stood in the north-west corner of the Cathedral nave, (entered through the west door, here with a wooden screen around it). When the church was built, there would have been blank windows at both sides in the west bay, as there were houses close to the west end of the church on both sides. The font is now immediately in front of the west door, and the monuments once on the wall had to be moved when the door was cut through; c1935. (JAW)
BELOW: The west bay of St Mary's Church projects beyong the wall of the Abbey precinct; early 20th century. (MS) RIGHT: Although, when he made his will in 1437, John Nottyngham left money to build porches at the south and west doors of St Mary's church, his executors extended the old north porch, the main entrance to the church before it was extended. The front of Nottyngham's porch is a fine piece of work, sadly in poor repair. (MS)

LEFT: The window on the east side of the Nottyngham porch is probably not contemporary with the north porch; although the tracery is in a style ealier than the porch front, it looks as if it has been altered. Some of the old prints suggest it once had moulding round it. Perhaps it is the work of Victorian restorers. (MS) BELOW: This unusual photograph of the Chapel of the Charnel dates from c1910. All the graves have since been removed from the area in front of the gate, and the elegant monument within the chapel is no longer there. (JAW) RIGHT: Tower Cottage, next to the Norman Tower, was designed by Cottingham and formed part of the Penny Bank group of buildings which are dated to 1846; before 1904. (JAW)

ABOVE: When this photograph was taken early this century, the area to the right of Shire Hall was used as part of the garden of the house called St Margaret's Gate, in Honey Hill, which the Town Trust hopes to rehabilitate in the near future. A tunnel under the road into the Churchyard connected the two parts of the garden. The Magpie Inn stood on the site of this garden until 1871. (MS)
BELOW: The Abbey House, Angel Hill, decorated for the Coronation of King George V in 1911. (JAW)

CIVIL LIBERTIES

A Mayor used to be an essentially urban figure, but that was changed by local government reorganisation in 1974, when boroughs like St Edmundsbury were created, which included large numbers of rural parishes as well as the town itself. Further changes may well be forthcoming as a result of the current review of local government.

Mayors are a relatively new introduction into Bury St Edmunds for, apart from a few years under Charles II and James II, Bury's first citizen was called the Alderman until 1836. The office appeared early in the town's history, and the right to have an Alderman became one of the main issues between Abbey and town. It has been suggested, with considerable justification, that in monastic times, the Alderman's first function was to act as champion of the townsmen against the might of the Abbey. Men of great ability and determination were required to fulfil this demanding role.

The office of Alderman first occurs in the early years of the 13th century and the first Alderman whose name is known was Wodard, son of Ely, who often witnessed charters. The Alderman of the town was then also Alderman of the guild merchant, an organisation of merchants which regulated the trading of Bury men, especially in markets and fairs other than the town's own. When the town lost the right to have a guild merchant after the revolt of 1327, perhaps after a break, the townsmen continued to elect an alderman. He was elected each year in the Guildhall, which was first the home of the guild merchant and, later, of Candlemas Guild, which emphasises that he was of the town rather than of the Abbey. It was irksome to the townsmen that, at Michaelmas, they must go into St Edmund's church and seek permission from the Abbot, or whichever of his subordinates was in charge in his absence, to elect an alderman, whose election could be rejected. It is no wonder that the right to elect the Alderman without interference was one of the main points of issue between Abbey and town. The Abbot's ratification of the person elected by the townsmen was by no means always forthcoming; Jankyn Smyth, the town's great benefactor, was one of those whose election was, on at least one occasion, not confirmed.

Yates printed a version of the oath taken by the Alderman, before the Sacrist at the High Altar of the Abbey Church. He swore that he would faithfully serve the office of Alderman in the sight of the Abbot and Convent and all their servants; that he would keep the peace to the best of his ability; that he would neither appropriate nor encroach upon anything which belonged to the Abbot and Convent, nor take upon himself anything that belonged to the office of Bailiff; that he would not procure himself, or through some other person, anything which might harm or damage the Abbot or Convent, but that he would be ready to defend them in all rights and customs that belonged to them. This reads as though the Alderman was to protect the rights of the Abbey against the demands of the townsmen, while the townsmen regarded the Alderman as their champion.

The office of Alderman no doubt involved those who held it in some expense, and there is evidence that the Alderman received an income from some properties. He appointed the St Mary Priest in St James's Church and also the priest of Robert of Eriswell's chantry in that church. In the absence of one of the Bailiffs (who were the Sacrist's officers) he could take his place in the town court, the Portmanmoot, which was held in the Toll House. Other duties included the appointment, subject to confirmation by the Sacrist, of watchmen and gatekeepers, and he had some responsibility for the military service required from the town. The collection, if not the assessment, of taxes levied upon the townsmen was another important duty. The execution of this duty may well have influenced Jankyn Smyth and other early benefactors of the town, who endowed charities to provide for the payment of town taxes.

The names of many of the pre-dissolution Aldermen are known, and they were all substantial men, reinforcing the impression gained from other sources that the Burgesses were an elite group of the wealthier townsmen. Surprisingly enough, in some years at least, it is known that an Alderman was elected in the interim period between the dissolution of the Abbey in 1539 and the incorporation of the Borough in 1606. It is not clear whether these men were regarded as the Alderman of Candlemas Guild, officially defunct but which survived to administer the town charities, or of the town. One of those who held the office then was Sir Nicholas Bacon, Lord Keeper of the Great Seal; he was Alderman 1573-1574.

The incorporation of the Borough in 1606 at last defined the duties of the Alderman, and set out the manner of his election which was to be followed, with only a short break, until 1836, when the Municipal Corporations Act of 1835 came into effect. The first charter of James I incorporated the town by the name of the Alderman and Burgesses of Bury St Edmunds, and provided for an Alderman, four Assistants, 12 Chief or Capital Burgesses and 24 Burgesses of the Common Council, and named the first members. The four Assistants were Justices of the Peace, who assisted the Alderman as Chief Magistrate of the town. The Alderman and Assistants were elected each year on the Thursday after St Bartholemew's Day, 24 August, and sworn in to their offices on the Thursday after Michaelmas. The Alderman and Assistants made their oaths to perform their offices before the Recorder or, in his absence, before one of the Capital Burgesses who had already served a term as Alderman. Often one or two gentlemen who lived in or near the town were elected Assistants, as well as some of the Capital Burgesses. The good government of Bury St Edmunds, and preserving law and order within its bounds, were the principal function of the Corporation. Members were to be chosen from among the freemen of the town, although the numbers of those admitted to the freedom gradually declined and eventually only those who were ambitious to hold civic office bothered to take it up. The Alderman and Assistants were to be elected in the presence of the inhabitants, surely indicating that the election meeting of the Corporation was regarded as a public meeting.

The Alderman as Chief Magistrate presided over the Borough Magistrate's court and, after 1614, sat with the Recorder at its own court of Quarter Sessions. He also held the Court of Record, which dealt with civil pleas, and the Court Leet which, before the creation of an organised police force, appointed the constables who patrolled the town, dealt with basic questions affecting public health and, an important function in a market town, investigated allegations of the use of false weights and measures. From 1614, when the privileges of the Borough were increased, the immediate past Alderman became, *ex officio*, the Coroner for the following year. Mr Alderman was also the Clerk of the Market, and responsible for its orderly conduct, and proclaimed the fairs and held the court of Pie Powder at which disputes between traders could be speedily resolved. The recently published diaries of James Oakes, who held the office of Alderman for several terms, show how the annual meetings to elect and swear in the Alderman, with their customary dinners and church services, punctuated the civic year.

Those elected to the office of Alderman were expected to take up the post and, should any one refuse to do this, the Corporate body fixed a fine which had to be paid. In times of crisis, the office had its drawbacks. Mr Alderman was no figurehead, and could not shirk his duties, be they ever so disagreeable. When the Corporation met on 17 August 1665 to elect an Alderman, Francis Godfrey was first elected, refused to accept the office, and was fined £35. Mr Edward Bourne was elected next, but he too refused and was fined £50. Thomas Macro was then elected, refused, and was fined £50, before Samuel Hustler eventually accepted office for the year. This was, of course, the great plague year in London, and anyone who undertook the office of Alderman of Bury St Edmunds in that year would be well aware that, had plague actually got into the town, however serious it became, he would have no chance of fleeing into the country where there would have been less likelihood of infection. The Edward Bourne who refused to serve in 1665 was the son of Edward Bourne whose name appears in the old lists of Aldermen under 1637, the year which can be called Bury St Edmund's great plague year. As the proceedings of the Corporation before 1652 are no longer among the Borough records, this cannot be checked but, if Edward Bourne was elected in August 1637, he could not have served his term, for he died in September that year, perhaps himself a plague victim. On occasions when law and order broke down, it was the Alderman who had to read the Riot Act.

The Alderman during these centuries had a real job to do, if only as the Chief Magistrate, for in Bury St Edmunds, as in many other towns, especially in the 18th century, the Corporation itself was frequently lacking in initiative and application to the problems of the town. As well as attendance in court, the Borough Magistrates were generally speaking 'on call' should a magistrate be required for a multitude of administrative as well as legal duties. The magistracy carried out, voluntarily, many administrative tasks which are now done by local government officers or civil servants.

Between 1684 and 1688 Bury St Edmunds was a Mayoral town, for the town was governed by a charter which provided for a governing body consisting of a Mayor, Alderman and Councillors. This was a difficult time for town corporations, as Charles II and then James II constantly removed members who did not support their religious policies and packed them with their own nominees under charters such as that issued to Bury St Edmunds. In Bury St Edmunds, and in many other towns, only the Corporation members — just 37 men — elected the town's two Members of

Parliament, and it was of the utmost importance to both Charles II and James II that the Boroughs would return men who would support them.

The reforms of the 19th century replaced the self-perpetuating oligarchy which had governed the town since 1606, with an elected council and, for almost the first time, officially introduced the office of Mayor. The first Mayor, in anything like the modern sense, was Francis King Eagle, who took office in January 1836 under the Municipal Corporations Act of the previous year. This legislation created uniformity by sweeping away ancient titles such as Alderman for a town's first citizen and, here and in other towns, elections were for a long time held on 9 November.

The 1606 charter had granted the right for two maces to be carried before the Alderman, and the number was increased to four in 1614. Records of the Corporation are scanty before 1652, but it can be assumed that maces had been provided long before 1668, when John Clarke was paid £45 for two. The earliest reference to civic insignia known is the payment, in 1615, of £7 2s 0d by the Guildhall Feoffees for the 'Towne Auncient' or banner. In the following year the Feoffees were spending heavily on a new council chamber at the Guildhall, for which they provided the Royal Arms and a portrait of James I, with the three charters, as well as portraits of Jankyn Smyth and Thomas Bright the elder, the two outstanding benefactors of the town. In 1622, the Feoffees also bought silver cognisances or badges for the town waits. The wearing of gowns by all members of the Corporation can also be assumed from the beginning. John Inman, who was described as one of the Burgesses in the burial register when he died in 1626, left his two 'hall goundes' to his brother-in-law, Richard Gooding, a merchant of Kings Lynn. The sword of state was given by Sir Thomas Hervey on 2 October 1664; Charles II's grant of the right to have a sword of state is squeezed in at the bottom of the charter of 3 July 1684. The Alderman's (now Mayor's) chain was given by James Oakes in 1805. It cost £140 and was made by Rundell, Bridge & Co. of Ludgate Hill.

Bury St Edmunds struggled long and hard for its municipal privileges. Civic occasions, when the Mayor wears his robes and is preceded by the sword of state and the maces, serve to remind us of a time when, even though a town was large and prosperous like medieval Bury St Edmunds, the granting of burghal status was by no means inevitable, especially in a town tightly controlled by a great magnate, as Bury was by the Abbot of St Edmunds. Nowadays the Mayor presides over meetings of the Council, but spends much time visiting organisations within St Edmundsbury. It would be sad if the civic pageantry were ever to be lost, for it ought to remind every one that civic liberties were once fought for in this town, and should be cherished and preserved.

OPPOSITE ABOVE: Owen Aly Clarke was Mayor in 1907-1908 and also throughout the First World War, here in the Banqueting Room in the Guildhall, which was then used as a Council Chamber. Mr Clarke is wearing the mayoral robe and cocked hat. The Mayor's chain was given by James Oakes in 1805, but the original medallion, which had the bust of James I on it, was replaced by one with the bust of William IV, in 1836. The Sword Bearer and Sergeants-at-Mace stand behind him with the symbols of Mayoral office. He is seated in the Mayor's chair which, with a council table and chairs for Councillors was bought in 1877, when it was decided that the Council could no longer meet in the old Council Chamber upstairs, at the back of the Guildhall. The furniture was made by a local firm, Bullen, whose shop was where Big Mac and Thomas Cook's are now; probably 1907.

LEFT: One of the early burials in the Cemetery was that of Francis King Eagle, the first Mayor after the passing of the Municipal Corporations Act. The memorial, in the form of an obelisk, was paid for by a public subscription and was designed, free of charge, by Mr Cooper of Cooper and Peck, the architects who designed the Cemetery chapels and lodge. (MS) RIGHT: A Freedom ceremony: the illuminated copy of the Freedom resolution is held by the last Recorder of Bury St Edmunds, who is wearing a full-bottomed wig. The office was abolished in 1972. (StE BC)

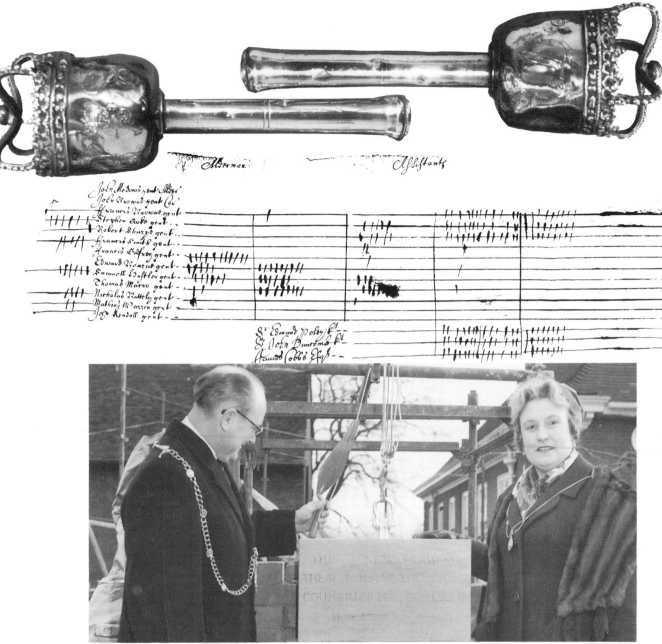

ABOVE: On incorporation in 1606, the right to have two maces was granted, but increased to four in 1614. The earliest reference to small maces dates from 1688, when an inventory included two great maces and two little maces. What has become of the little maces? Perhaps they were worn out by 1715, when Thomas Rainsford, surgeon, Alderman that year, presented a pair of small maces. In 1836, Abraham Gall, the last Alderman, attempted to retain the insignia and plate, no doubt in a last ditch attempt to pay off some debts of the unreformed Corporation. The two little maces and the common seal were the first items to be handed over to the new Council, on the grounds that they would be required; this suggests that then the little maces were used more frequently than the large ones. More recently, one of these maces somehow became detached from the rest of the insignia, but in 1974 it was spotted at a London antiques fair and was eventually bought from a West Country antique dealer. (PS) CENTRE: Voting paper for Alderman and Assistant Justices, 17 August 1665, the Great Plague Year; there was great reluctance to take office then as, if the plague had come to Bury St Edmunds, the Alderman would have had to stay in the town to discharge his office. (StE BC at SRO(B)) BELOW: Councillor Eric Steele, with Mrs Steele, lays the foundation stone of the Borough Offices extension, 11 February, 1966. (StE BC and BFP)

The Borough Council met for the last time at the Guildhall in December 1966. The earliest datable feature of the Guildhall is the inner entrance arch of c1250, and the earliest references to Guildhall Street come from about that time too. Thus, for over 700 years until 1966, this building had been used for considering matters bearing on the 'common profit and benefit of the town of Bury St Edmunds'. The Mayor in 1966 was Cllr. J. W. H. Knight. (StE BC and OGJ)

ABOVE: When the contents of St Andrews Castle were sold by Messrs Lacy Scott on 7, 8 and 9 July 1927, Lot 588 was described in their catalogue as 'An unusual set of the early Queen Anne period Dining Room Chairs, comprising arm chair and twelve others, made of walnut with cabriole legs and rush seats. These chairs were made for the Clopton Hospital, erected and endowed by Poley Clopton, M.D., 1730, an asylum for six poor men and six poor women who have paid Scot and Lot without having received parochial relief'. They sold for 245 guineas. From the inventory, made when the Hospital opened, they must have been the thirteen chairs in the Governors' Room, in which the Governors or Trustees met for their quarterly meetings. (LS) BELOW: The central part of Provost's House, built as Clopton's Hospital c1735, shows the coat of arms of Dr Poley Clopton in the pediment and the inscription above the door which was carved by Thomas Singleton in 1750 for 12 guineas. (MS)

THE MASTER BUILDERS

The Trustees of Clopton's Hospital, now the Provost's House, kept detailed building accounts which show those who were involved in building and furnishing one of Bury St Edmunds' Grade I listed buildings. The Steggles, father and son, often built houses in an easily recognisable style and, working from known examples of their work, similar buildings, if they were speculative ventures, and not commissioned by a client, can often be shown to be their work from the Rate Books. The De Carle family of stone masons and builders were the Steggles' contemporaries and, no doubt, rivals. Some of their business records survive and, with patience, it is possible to match some of the work recorded in their day books with tomb-stones or door cases which survive to this day.

Clopton's Hospital was built on part of the Abbey site, which the Trustees bought from Sir Jermyn Davers in 1735 for £62. The site consited of approximately half an acre, being 198 feet in length from east to west and 110 feet from north to south. Both the Trustees' minutes and accounts have survived and were immaculately kept, the first two Clerks to the Trustees being the two Thomas Warrens, best known as surveyors, though they described themselves as schoolmasters, and who themselves deserve a few lines. The elder Thomas, who died in 1762, made the plan of the town first published in 1747. His son, who lived until 1815, brought out a second edition of his father's map in 1776, on which a few revisions were made, but is chiefly known now for his survey of the whole town, not just the built-up area, of which the original is in Moyses Hall Museum, and of which there are photographs in the Athenaeum and other town buildings.

Although much of the work was paid for in 1735, and the Court of Chancery approved the schemes for the Hospital in 1737, the first residents did not move in until 1744. The 'main contractor' was obviously Thomas Steel, bricklayer, who also worked on the Manor House, which faces Clopton's Hospital across the Churchyard. He was initially paid £1,073 1s 6d. John Goodwin, the carpenter, was paid £556 7s 8d, Mr Singleton, the stone cutter, £139, 7s 0d and Mr Jaye, the plumber, £58 4s 0d. As the time approached for the residents to move in, payments for linen and other furnishings were made, as well as relatively small additional sums for builder's work. A payment of 15 guineas was made to Peter Lathbury 'for surveying the work at the Hospital'. This may relate only to the supervision of the building work, but in the days before there was any recognised architectural profession, could it be that Lathbury designed this building? Many members of the Lathbury family were artistic and Peter may well have had architectural ability.

Two items in the accounts of the Hospital are tantalising. They relate to the making of chairs. In 1927, Messrs Lacy Scott sold the contents of St Andrews Castle and one of the lots consisted of 'the Clopton chairs'. There were 13 chairs, in the Queen Anne style, twelve single and one with arms. From an inventory of the

Hospital, which was made when it opened, it is known that there were thirteen chairs in the Governors' room, in which the Trustees of the Hospital met. Elsewhere in the house there were a total of 28 chairs. Sadly the maker of these chairs cannot be determined as Richard Newman was paid £3 0s 0d for sixteen chairs on 8 December 1744 and John Shipman was paid £9 6s 0d for an unspecified number of chairs on 25 January 1745. Unless the chairs used by the Trustees were a gift — and, had that been the case, surely thanks would have been recorded in the minutes — one of these gentlemen made elegant chairs indeed.

The original wooden gates at the front of the house were ordered to be replaced by iron ones in 1749. In May 1750, Thomas Singleton was employed to put up the coat of arms and motto of the founder of the Hospital upon the pediment, with an inscription on a marble tablet over the Hall door. The cost was not to exceed £12 0s 0d. Over the years, many other well-known tradesmen were employed about the Hospital; William Steggles carried out roof repairs at the west end of the building in 1827. Mr Darkins was responsible for enlarging the building in 1841, when the Charity Commissioners insisted that the number of residents should be increased to sixteen.

Thomas Singleton, who carved the arms on the pediment of Clopton's Hospital, did much work in the town. His father, Robert, was a monumental sculptor of great ability, though it is thought that there are no examples of his work here in Bury St Edmunds. Thomas Singleton's best known work in the town is the Market Cross, where his carving is of a high quality. The Singletons lived in the house in Honey Hill, now called St Denys, which has a stone front, no doubt to advertise their skill in such work. The business passed into the hands of the De Carle family, and is now represented by Hanchets.

Robert De Carle, who worked between 1795 and 1842, is probably best known locally for the obelisk erected in memory the Earl Bishop in Ickworth Park in 1804. Their clients included many of the familiar local families — Oakes, Affleck, Hasted, Cullum — and more of the first families are represented only by the names of their estates — for example, Coldham, Culford, Livermere, Ickworth and Saxham. From time to time work took the family away from Bury St Edmunds and there is evidence of journeys to Stamford, Buckingham, Cambridge and above all into Hertfordshire, where they were contractors for the East India Company's College at Haileybury, 1806-1809. Day Books survive for a number of years. Much of their work related to paving the streets of the town, and they supplied many of their customers with garden rollers, as well as repairing their door steps. Often there are sketches of fireplaces or doorways which they were to make for their customers, and, given research to identify customers with houses, there is little doubt that in time it will be possible to identify some of this work. Their work as monumental masons provided a good bread-and-butter trade. In 1792 a 'head and feet stone in Memory of J. Halsted' was charged at £1 4s 0d and, in the same year, an altar tomb cost twelve guineas. Some entries refer to exchanging head and feet stones; was it then the custom for families to replace stones as they became worn and illegible? Letters on inscriptions were charged at 1d each. Other work was of a most mundane nature. When Clopton's Asylum, as it was called from 1825, was being extended in 1841, the De Carles were subcontractors to Mr Darkins for work connected with the well and they were also called upon to stop up rats' burrows at the Angel.

Those who wish to see some of the work of the De Carles, the Steggles and Mr Darkins, should spend some time in the Churchyard, discovering and deciphering the signatures on the monuments. (All those on headstones are now probably beneath ground level.) In the space of a few yards, by the side of the main walk from Samson's Tower to the Shire Hall, you can find examples of them all.

From 1959 until 1978, the author lived in a house built by William Steggles in 1834, and on stylistic grounds it is likely that her present house, which retains part of a 16th century frame, was, like many more in the town, 'given a face lift' by the Steggles, perhaps while Humphrey Steggles was landlord of the Three Crowns next door. The Steggles family of builders have left their mark on the appearance of Bury St Edmunds more than most. When Richard Payne surveyed the town in 1833, William Steggles owned more houses than anyone else. The name has been common in the area for a long time, and there are still members of the family living in the town. That was when the population was rising and there was a considerable demand for small terraced houses, which the firm built, and then rented rather than sold. It was also a period when anyone who was anyone wanted to have a house which, at least, looked as though it was built of stone. There is no good building stone in East Anglia and stucco was little used in Bury St Edmunds, but the Steggles — and other local builders — exploited the lovely creamy colour of white Woolpit brick and faced many much older houses with these bricks so that when they were new they did — or, if they have been cleaned in recent years, they do — look quite like stone fronted houses.

Three Steggles family tombs stand proudly in the Churchyard, overlooking Crown Street. One is to the first William, who was born c1742 and died on 21 May 1834, and his wife, Mary, who died aged 77 on 26 January 1832. In this William's will he was described as a bricklayer and made his mark, so he may have been illiterate. He had two sons, William II and Humphrey, and a daughter Mary Ann, who were living at the time of his death, and he made provision for the sons of his deceased son Zechariah. A large square tomb has an inscription on the west side, facing Crown Street, to William II, c1777-1859, and his wife Maria, who died in 1851 aged 72.

A William Steggles was listed as a builder in directories from 1823-1839, usually at 10 Whiting Street; it is likely that Churchgate Street in Pigot's *General Directrory "A"*, 1830, was an error. His business as a statuary and mason was carried on from Looms Lane until 1839, then from Brentgovel Street; perhaps they had a corner property. 1839 marked the zenith of the firm's activities when Pigot's *Directory* listed Steggles and Sons as brick makers, bricklayers, builders, statuaries, lime burners and land surveyors and Robson's *Directory,* also published in 1839, added stone and marble merchants to their activities. William II is not listed in White's *Directory* of 1844, but Susan Steggles, the widow of his son, William Henry, was listed as a bricklayer, builder, dealer in Woolpit brick and tiles, stone and marble mason and statuary at 17 Whiting Street. This information is also given in Kelly's *Directory*, 1846, with William back as a builder in Whiting Street. Slater's *Suffolk Dirctory 1850* lists among the builders Susan Steggles, at 16½ Whiting Street, and William at 10

Whiting Street, and in *White's Directory*, 1855, Mr William Steggles was listed as living at 11 Whiting Street and a James Steggles, joiner and builder, was at 20 Whiting Street. The *Post Office Directory*, 1858, lists only Frederick Steggles, mason, at 16½ Whiting Street.

It is clear from the records of the Guildhall Feoffees that William Steggles — presumably William I — leased the property in Whiting Street (which is now Model Junction) on a repairing lease for 25 years in 1806; William II gave up the premises in 1842, but a further lease of this property was granted to him in 1846. Richard Payne's survey of the town made in 1833 described this property, then 10 Whiting Street, as consisting of a house, workshop, lodges, counting house, chaise house, stables and yards containing 1 rood 4 perches. From the entries in the various directories, it is obvious that the business was run from these premises, with another yard in Looms Lane or Brentgovel Street.

Payne's survey of 1833 gives a good idea of the Steggles' property interests at that time, and shows that he had quite a holding near the corner of Whiting Street and Churchgate Street. Steggles himself owned nos 11 and 12 Whiting Street, after which came one house and then the Mason's Arms. After the Mason's Arms he owned nos 15 and 16 Whiting Street, as well as all the property in Churchgate Street from the corner of Whiting Street to the Unitarian Chapel. He had acquired the Churchgate Street property in 1828 and immediately proceeded to build the present properties there. These and some other properties, which are known to have been built or remodelled by Steggles, are shown in the photographs. Some of Steggles' humbler houses have been 'slum cleared' in recent years. This has happened to part of Cannon Place, which originally had 23 houses with gardens. All that remains is the row across the end of Pea Porridge Green which connects Church Row with Cannon Street. However, there are stones inscribed 'W.S. 1825' on both ends of the surviving buildings, with the name Cannon Place at the Cannon Street end, and a stone on the Church Row end, reading 'age 79'. Cannon Place must have been built by William I, who died in 1834.

The earliest identified building by the Steggles is Long Row, Southgate Street, a block of Almshouses, which were designed and built for the Guildhall Feoffees, in 1811, at a cost of £300. Improvement in recent years has left little apart from the walls that is original. The former William Barnaby Almshouses in College Street were also rebuilt according to Steggles' plan and specification, in 1826, as a cost of £1256. The firm usually undertook repairs to the properties owned by the Feoffees; for instance, in 1833 payments amounting to over £668 were made for work carried out by them at the Angel. William II substantially improved the Feoffees' house on the corner of the south side of Churchgate Street and Guildhall Street in 1847.

Although the Steggles used a great deal of white Woolpit brick, they did from time to time use red brick. Payne's 1833 survey shows that William Steggles owned seven houses on the west side of St John's Street immediately before the Friends' Meeting House as one walks from the Market Place. There are still three or four Steggles style houses next to the Meeting House, but they are built in red brick. The others were no doubt demolished when the old Bury St Edmunds Police Station was built in 1892.

For several years after 1839 William II was in financial difficulties and the Eastern Counties Bank was managing his affairs and paying dividends to his creditors.

However, he seems to have weathered the storm and continued to work for the Guildhall Feoffees and, no doubt, others, almost to the end of his long life. William II's disappearance from the 1844 *Directory* and the gap in his tenancy of the Whiting Street property must have resulted from his financial troubles.

An example of the Steggles work as statuaries is the marble tablet in memory of James Oakes, d1828, in the north-west corner of the Lady Chapel in St Mary's church. A number of monuments signed Steggles can be found in the Churchyard.

ABOVE: The carving on the Market Cross is the best known work of Thomas Singleton in Bury St Edmunds. BELOW: St Denys in Honey Hill was the home first of the Singletons and afterwards of the De Carles. Its stone facade was undoubtedly a form of advertisement for the skill of those who lived there. (MS)

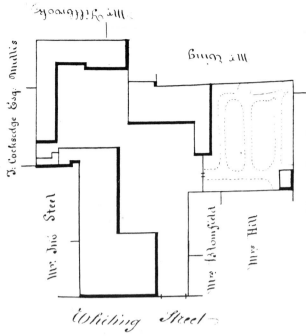

LEFT: It was from these premises, which they leased from the Guildhall Feoffees, that the Steggles ran their business. (MS)
RIGHT: A plan of the premises occupied by Mr Steggles from J. G. Lenny's plan, 1822. (GFT at SRO(B)) BELOW: The remaining part of Cannon Place, built by William Steggles I in 1825. (MS)

LEFT: These houses in St John's Street were built by Steggles, using red rather than white brick. (MS) RIGHT: 81 and 82 Risbygate Street were built by Steggles in 1834. (MS) BELOW: 3 and 4 Chequer Square are old houses remodelled by Steggles. William II's daughter had a school at number 3 in 1839, while his son Edward, a druggist, had his business at number 4 in 1844. (MS)

LEFT: Although no evidence has been found directly linking William Steggles with these houses in Chequer Square, when the Paving Commissioners objected to the projecting balconies in 1840, they negotiated with the Eastern Counties Bank, who had taken over Steggles' assets when he found himself in financial difficulty in 1839. (MS) CENTRE: A stable and garden, valued at only £5 for rating purposes, stood on the site of 81 and 82 Whiting Street until 1812, when Steggles had built two new houses, which were then unoccupied. In 1814 they were valued at £15 each. (MS) BELOW: This terrace in Whiting Street is described as belonging to William Steggles in Payne's Survey of 1833. (MS) RIGHT: In 1815 the Guildhall Feoffees acquired the house which had belonged to Mrs Bloomfield, and which adjoined the back of the Guildhall; Steggles converted it into a residence for the Hall Keeper and an office for the Clerk Receiver. This is Steggle's plan for this property, with his signature, (c1815). (GFT at SRO(B))

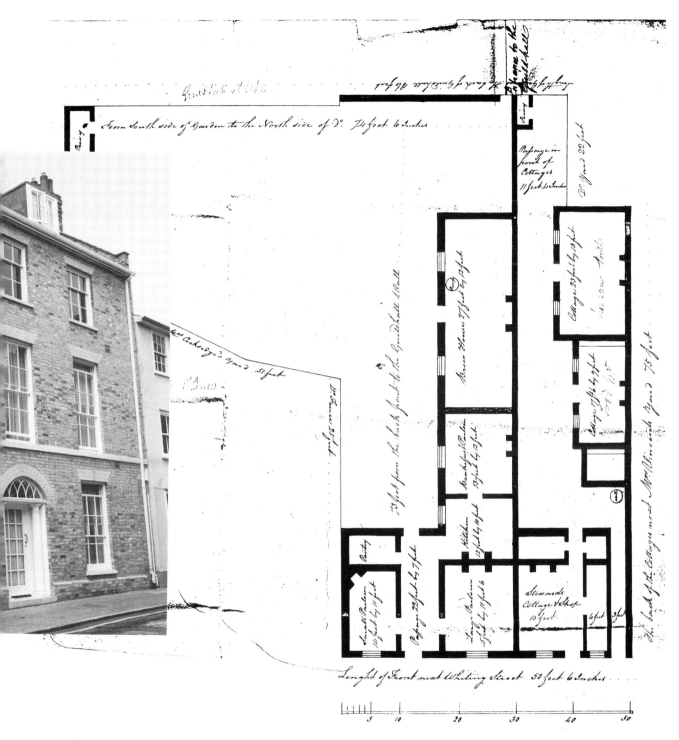

The Ground Plan of Mr. Blomfields House Garden and Yard. Whiting Street Bury. — Willm Steggles

LEFT: These houses in Hatter Street belonged to Steggles before 1833. (MS) RIGHT: Steggles rented this property from the Feoffees on a repairing lease (and presumably sub-let it) for many years before he refronted it in 1849. In that year the Feoffees decided that in time all their houses should be given brick fronts. (MS) BELOW: Steggles acquired the site of these houses, between the corner of Whiting Street and the Unitarian Meeting House, in 1828. (MS)

ABOVE: The tomb of Alice De Carle who died in 1818. (MS) LEFT: Like the Singletons before them, the Hanchets, who eventually bought the De Carle business, ran theirs from a stone-faced building. (MS) RIGHT: The last memorial to William and Mary Steggles is their joint tomb — appropriately in stone. (MS)

ABOVE: Instead of distributing shillings to the Almshouse residents during the Commemoration service, the Trustees now entertain the residents to lunch after the service: the Chairman, the Very Rev Raymond Furnell, Provost of St Edmundsbury, the Warden, Mrs Kate Davies, Mrs Adelaide Borley and Mrs Sherril Furnell, 18 June 1992. (MS) BELOW: Edward Bourne and other members of his family are commemorated by these tombs, which are the oldest remaining in the Great Churchyard. (MS)

108

FOR SOULS IN NEED

Charities began with those gifts which pre-Reformation testators made to speed their souls through purgatory. These often took the form of bequests for masses to be sung or other prayers. Often bequests were made towards the cost of building work which was going on in the testator's parish church, or he or she might leave money to buy vestments or some other ornament. This makes medieval wills a vital source for the history of church building, as wills from a parish often chart the progress of work on its church. Jankyn Smyth, Bury's most outstanding benefactor, had built the chancel aisles and sanctuary of St Mary's Church during his lifetime, but we know this only because, when he made his will, he provided for their upkeep. Other bequests which were considered charitable and of benefit to the testator's soul might be for the relief of the poor, the repair of highways or for payment of taxes which fell on the community as a whole.

For over 500 years, the Guildhall Feoffees have administered funds intended to relieve the inhabitants of the town from various hardships. (For all practical purposes, a Feoffee can be regarded as equivalent to a trustee). Jankyn Smyth's bequest to the town, which came into effect upon his death in 1481, was to help pay taxes imposed upon the town by its monastic overlords. Margaret Odeham who, like Jankyn Smyth, had set up her charity in 1470, did not die until 1492, when her gift for helping prisoners in Bury Gaol came into being. Others followed the example of these two by either making a gift for some immediate need or by adding to the endowment administered by the Feoffees. More recently, the Feoffees, under Charity Commissioners' Schemes, have become responsible for a number of charities which originally had their own feoffees or trustees, although, of course, some of the town charities, such as Dr Clopton's Charity, still have their own administrative arrangements.

Quite a lot of those who helped build up the endowment established by Jankyn Smyth and Margaret Odeham have themselves been Feoffees. This was true of Adam Newhawe in the 15th century, John Salter and William Tassell in the 16th and Thomas Bright and Francis Pynner in the 17th. The 18th and 19th century Feoffees do not seem to be represented among the benefactors and indeed, during these centuries there were far fewer benefactors. However, in recent years, two ladies who were active Feoffees, Eva Pauline Greene, who was the first woman to become Mayor of Bury St Edmunds, and Joyce Ella Cockram, a well-loved doctor in the town, left legacies to the Trust.

For the first century or so all the Feoffees were members of the influential Candlemas Guild. Its admission fees and membership charges ensured that only the wealthier residents of the town could aspire to membership. Although, of course, only men appear as Feoffees at this early date, women could, and did, join religious guilds of this kind. Margaret Odeham was one of them. From her will, which is the only source of personal information about her, she appears to have been a sociable lady, fond of good, fashionable clothes, but nevertheless mindful of the needs of others, especially, in her case, of the prisoners in the town goal, which in the fifteenth century was on Cornhill, roughly where the Electricity Board showroom is now. Margaret Odeham was the third wife of her husband, John, who died over twenty years before she did. By the time she died, both their daughters were dead too. It is quite clear that she enjoyed good relations with her two sons-in-law, one of whom had remarried before her death. Had there been any grandchildren they would undoubtedly have been left something. Lack of heirs is one factor which probably influenced a number of benefactors. Sometimes testators left a residuary bequest to the Feoffees, which was only to take effect if their heirs died out.

Because the first Feoffees were all members of Candlemas Guild, and especially as the Guild altered its statutes long before the death of either Jankyn Smyth or Margaret Odeham, it seems inevitable that the Guild should have discussed those hardships which members might best relieve. Jankyn Smyth's bequest was primarily for payment of town taxes; as one who had been Alderman on several occasions he would have been aware of the problems of collecting taxes from the townsmen, especially those who were not well off. Taxation was a sore point in 15th century Bury St Edmunds, as various impositions were laid on the town by the Abbey, in addition to the usual Royal taxes which everyone paid.

One early bequest which is perplexing is that of Sir John Frenze, the Master of St Peter's Hospital in Out Risbygate, who left land to provide for the relief of lepers. The Hospital of which he was master was itself a leper hospital, which had been founded by Abbot Anselm, who ruled from 1121-1148; had its endowments become inadequate?

Because to a greater or lesser extent the charitable causes supported by the bequest of Jankyn Smyth, Margaret Odeham and other early benefactors came to be regarded as 'superstitious' — that is, that they provided for such things as masses for the dead or the support of chantry priests — some of the early endowments were confiscated by the Crown during the reign of King Edward VI. In most, perhaps all, cases the Feoffees were able to buy back the land concerned, largely because the plate and treasures which had belonged to the two parish churches were sold before they could be confiscated by the Crown. They also acquired some property which had not previously been their concern. It was then that the Feoffees acquired their estate at Hepworth, with which Jankyn Smyth had endowed his chantry in St Mary's Church and which had been run quite independently of the Feoffees until that time. All these lands became known as the New Purchased Lands. Sir John Cullum's copy of the 18th century catalogue of benefactors, which used to be read out each year at the Commemoration Service, quite rightly included Sir Nicholas Bacon, Queen Elizabeth I's Lord Keeper of the Great Seal, Sir Clement Heigham, who was Speaker of the House of Commons under Queen Mary and Sir Ambrose Jermyn 'and other gentlemen of the Feoffment [who] were the Means to procure a better conveyance of those houses and lands, which otherwise might have been lost. And therefore they are Deservedly Commemorated amongst Our Worthy Benefactors'. Another prominent man, certainly a member of Candlemas Guild and on at least one occasion one of its auditors, was Stephen Gardiner, Bishop of Winchester and Lord Chancellor under Queen Mary, who maintained friendly relations with his home town and may well have been prepared to help in ensuring that the people of Bury retained some benefit from such lands. During the reigns of the three children of Henry VIII, Bury St Edmunds had many friends in places from which they could exert influence on behalf of the town.

It seems likely that the then Feoffees encouraged those who bought former almshouses and similar property, which had been confiscated by the Crown, to convey such property to them so that they could continue to be used for their original purpose. By 1433, if not earlier, there were almshouses under the Abbey wall in Crown Street which, until they were demolished in 1813, filled most of the site between the houses near the Norman Tower and St Mary's Church. These were conveyed to the Feoffees by Bartholemew Brockesby in 1564. Another case where this happened is the former William Barnaby almshouses, which have recently been converted into town houses. The original buildings on this site formed part of the College of Jesus, which was founded by Jankyn Smyth to provide a residence for the priests of St Mary's and St James's. As well as the College itself, the complex included six tenements, two of which were to be let, while the other four provided homes for four poor old men. These were bought by William Barnaby who, with his wife, Lady Fitzwarren, a daughter of Sir Thomas Kytson the elder of Hengrave Hall, lived in the Manor House at Great Saxham. He bought this and other property from the Crown and then conveyed the almshouses to the Feoffees in 1570. (Although writers on Bury St Edmunds, such as Tymms, state that the College stood on the west side of College Street where the Telephone Exchange and some town houses are now, recent research suggests that its site was on the opposite side of the street, on the south side of the turn into Church Walks.)

After the Reformation, testators ceased to leave bequests for masses and other superstitious uses; bequests to the Feoffees became more and more concerned with the relief of the poor as the sixteenth century wore on. One of the town's problems was increasing unemployment as the decline of the clothmaking industry, immigration into the town from the surrounding villages and an increasing birthrate combined to create widespread hardship. Sir Edmund Jermyn, whose handsome portrait still hangs with those of other benefactors in the Guildhall, left £40 a year out of the manor of Torksey in Lincolnshire to provide a stock of materials which could give work to poor people. Several other benefactors, like Richard Walker and Edward Bourne, looked to this way of relieving poverty caused by unemployment.

Thomas Bright the elder, who died in 1587, directed that his residuary estate should be divided equally between his surviving children and the charity. This amounted to the then large sum of £300, which was used to buy clothes for a considerable number of poor people. Thomas Bright is another benefactor whose picture hangs in the Guildhall. Spiritual as well as physical needs were provided by some of the town's benefactors. One of these was Edward Darby who, when he died in 1631, gave £300 for a public catechising in St James's Church. His monument, erected by his brother Henry, can still be seen on the wall of the south aisle. With the £300, lands of the annual value of £17 6s 8d were to be purchased and the money used for 'catechiseing once every fortnight of the poore in St James' parish; 13s. 4d. being allowed for every catechize, whereof ten groates shall be to the Minister, and the other 10s. shall be for 70 loaves of Wheat Bread, 65 are to be for so many poor people who are catechised, the remaining five loaves for the Clerk and Sexton'.

Sometimes the oddest circumstances led to the creation of a small charity, a particularly attractive one being Robert Browne's apprenticing charity. His will explained that the Burgesses of Bury St Edmunds had been indebted to him for £10 ever since he had last been Alderman 'for theire dinners at severall times and for other expences laid out by me whilest I was last Alderman by theire appointment and procurement as hath usually been paid to former Aldermen as by a note under their or some of their hands appeareth' and that he wished the money to be used to bind out poor children apprentices, two every year in each parish. There were other benfactors, such as Dorothy Calthorpe, who provided for apprenticing young men. When she made her will in 1693, she left money for this purpose to the Corporation, who used it to buy the Falcon Inn (now Ann Johnson's, the hairdresser's) in Chequer Square. After the Municipal Corporations Act of 1835, the administration of this and the other corporate charities was transferred to the Feoffees.

By the 19th century many of the objects for which the charities had originally been endowed had become irrelevant. Under a scheme of the Charity Commissioners in 1842 much of the Feoffees' considerable endowment was used to set up the Guildhall Feoffment Schools which had a marked influence on the town before the introduction of compulsory state education. Today, this five hundred year old organisation is mainly an almshouse charity which provides homes for about forty elderly people in four blocks of almshouses, although a certain amount of money is available for relief of need, and for educational purposes. In recent years it has been possible to help the unit for the profoundly deaf at the County Upper School, and to help young people setting out on a career. As people now live longer and are generally healthier, the present Feofees have identified a need for provision for the frail elderly who are not ill, but need extra help with normal everyday living. The Trustees have a site in Chalk Road where such a unit could be built as soon as funding is available from the Housing Corporation — unless there is a twentieth century benefactor who could expedite the scheme.

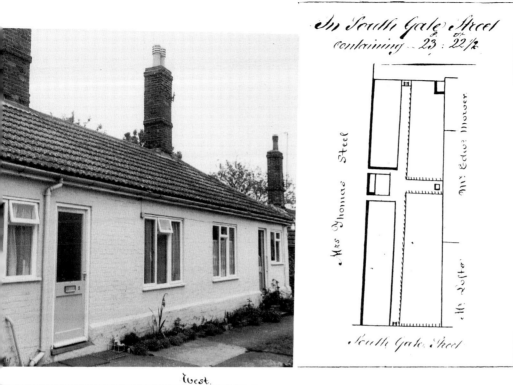

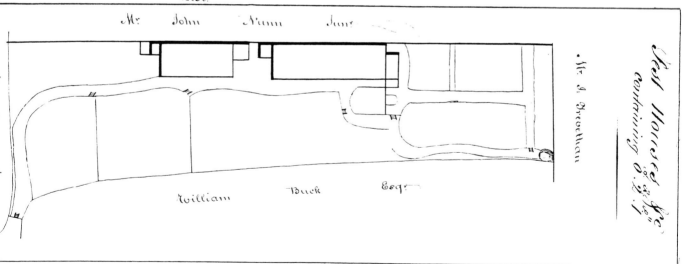

LEFT: Part of Long Row, Southgate Street; designed and built for the Feoffees by William Steggles in 1811, constant adaptation and modernisation have deprived the buildings of almost all the details set out in the specification. (MS) RIGHT: Plan of Long Row, Southgate Street, by J. G. Lenny, 1822, (GFT at SRO(B)) and BELOW: plan of the Pest Houses, also by J. G. Lenny, 1822. The Pest Houses were built in 1665, the Great Plague Year in London. Fortunately the plague did not reach Bury St Edmunds that year, but they were later used during many smallpox epidemics. (GFT at SRO(B))

ABOVE: College Square, the main block of Almshouses, built in 1909. (MS) CENTRE: Long Row, Northgate Street, built 1912. (MS) BELOW: Jankyn's Place, Chalk Road, built in 1939 to replace old almshouses in other parts of the town. It was intended that in time almshouses should be built round three sides of the site in the traditional manner, but this never happened because of the outbreak of war. The Trustees plan to built a frail care unit on part of this site as soon as funds can be found. (MS)

THERE IS A TAVERN

It seems certain that there must have been far more inns in medieval Bury St Edmunds than appear in surviving documents. If this is not a sufficient handicap, inns often changed their names, and there are instances of successful landlords taking their signs with them when they moved to larger premises.

A survey of property which had once belonged to the Abbey, made in 1580, reveals relatively few properties which seem to have been inns. On the north side of Horsemarket (St Mary's Square), where St Mary's Vicarage is now, was a tenement lately called the Pye. Pye Lane was then the name of the present Prussia Lane. In Crown Street was the Cheker, which no doubt gave its name to Chequer Square. This inn seems to be the same as that which was called the Falcon when John Baret made his will in 1463. Under the Guildhall Street heading there was the Pye, and the Saracens Head, which is now the British Legion Club. On Angel Hill there was a house which had formerly been called the White Hart, which can probably be identified with the Hert at Hoop which is known to have belonged to John Baret, who died in 1467, and his father, who died in 1416. A property on the south side of Cook Row — somewhere opposite the present Corn Exchange — had formerly been called the Swan. Within the Great Market the Moone, which must be the later Half Moon, the galleries of which are hidden within W.H. Smith's shop, is recorded as well as the Greyhound (from which the Pittancer received £5 6s 8d rent when the Abbey was dissolved in 1539); this inn was renamed the Suffolk Hotel in the 19th century. Abuttals to property provide references to the Maidenhead, which may have been in either Garland Street or Lower Baxter Street, and the Bull, which is known to have stood on the site of the Borough Offices. Under the heading of Brentgovel Street there were references to the Kings Head *alias* the Crown and to the White Horse which stood on the 'Bus Station site, where Clinton's Cards are now. In that part of Mustow (Angel Hill) which was in St James' parish there was a property which had formerly been known as the Saddle, as well as the Bull, already mentioned. The Woolpack in the High Street (Northgate Street) sounds like an inn, but the Parlour in Northgate Street may well have just been a private house. In 1539 the Prior had a property called the Boar's Head somewhere in the town, which certainly sounds as though it was an inn. The intriguingly named Alderman's Hall in the Spicer Row and Barber Row section of Abbeygate Street, Skeldhall, in Crown Street, and le Leshall, which was in School Hall Street (now Honey Hill or Raingate Street) were probably not inns. Moyses Hall, for which there is a well-known reference to rioters breakfasting there in 1328, may, for a time at least, have been an inn, but the evidence is far from conclusive.

Those who can be said without any hestitation to have owned inns in medieval Bury St Edmunds were wealthy men. The first of the former rent payers noted in the 1433 rental for the Angel, although its name is not given in that document, was Robert of Paston. He can be found paying tax in 1327 and 1340 and was one of the wealthiest men in the town at the time. Of 154 taxpayers in Bury St Edmunds in 1327, who paid amounts ranging from 1s 0d to 10s 0d, two paid 10s 0d, one 9s 0d, two 8s 0d and five, one of whom was Robert of Paston, who paid 7s 0d, all the others paying smaller sums. In 1340 he was taxed for 38 acres of land, with few owning more than he did. The amount of tax paid is not noted in Robert Paston's case. Some people paid 3s 4d for their 9th for ten acres, but most of those with about 30 acres seem to have paid 10s. He was not among those who were required to pay a 15th on their moveable goods. Deeds in the British Library show that he owned land without the West Gate and elsewhere in the fields of Bury St Edmunds. In one of these deeds he was a *Tabebarius*, taverner or inn keeper. Baret and his son, John, whose own wealth is denoted by what remains of his chantry chapel in St Mary's Church and from his gift to that church of the Angels of the Canopy, if not the whole of the Angel roof, owned an inn called the Hert of Hoop, probably the later White Hart, in Mustowe (Angel Hill or Mustow Street). John Baret also refers to a house known as the Falcon, which adjoined his own house in Chequer Square, which also seems to have belonged to him. Early in the 17th century Francis Pynner, a rich grocer, owned the Greyhound, now the Suffolk, the Bear and the Golden Bushell. (It is likely that the licence to rebuild an inn in the Butter Market which had been destroyed in the fire in 1608, granted to Pynner by the Alderman and Burgess in 1611, related to the Suffolk.) Although Francis Pynner described himself as a grocer, he had a licence to draw wine at the Greyhound, which he left to his daughter, Joyce, and another licence to draw wine in Mildenhall, which he left to his grandson, Valentine Elsden. Men such as these are unlikely to have concerned themselves with the day-to-day running of an inn, and it is probable that a tenant ran it, perhaps combining that with another trade. In 1433 those who paid rent for the properties which were to become the Angel were Robert Cole, a butcher, and John Cote, skinner.

The Angel is better documented than most inns as it was for a long time owned by the Guildhall Feoffees, whose records have survived quite well. As it formed part of the Sacrist land holding, it can also be traced in the rentals of 1433 and 1526.

The earliest surviving deed of the Angel, which is dated 8 May 1417, relates to only part of the site of the present Hotel, which was an inn called the Castle with a messuage called le Cookery, and a messuage 'once of Roger Rose' annexed to the tenement. There is a much fuller description of the property in the next deed in the series, a conveyance made on 20 July 1525 from William a More of Bury St Edmunds, yeoman, and Crystian, his wife, to Thomas Powle, eldest son of Thomas Powle of Bury St Edmunds, for the sum of £133 13s 4d. The property involved was the Angel itself. It extended from Mustowe (Angel Hill) through to Old Baxter Street (Angel Lane). To the south of the Angel was a tenement which had formerly been called the *Sarysynshed*, which also belonged to William a More while he also owned a tenement on the north side of the inn, which he had bought from Richard Copynger. Once again, we are able to compare this information with that to be found in the Sacrist's rental of 1526. By 1530, Thomas Powle was in financial difficulties and the Angel was mortgaged to Thomas Jermyn of Rushbrook. When Thomas Powle the elder made his will on 20 February 1531 he left the messuage or tenement in which he lived, called the Angel, with the tenements late adjoining which he had bought from William and Christian More to his master, Thomas Jermyn. Powle also left Master

Jermyn those moveable goods at the Angel, which were specified in an inventory to which his master was privy, in satisfaction of £50 which Jermyn had paid on behalf of the testator to 'my lord Burgeny for myn Office'. The exact nature of the office and the part of Lord Burgeny, who owned property in the town in the 16th century, remains to be investigated.

Sir Thomas Jermyn was paying customary rents for the Angel during the decade between the dissolution of the Abbey and the dissolution of the guilds and chantries in 1549, but on 1 April in the latter year he alienated the property to Nicholas Plat, a citizen and salter of London. On this occasion the property was described as two messuages, one called the Angel and the other the Castle, which had belonged to Thomas Powle and before that to William Moore. South of this block of property was a tenement belonging to James Jankynson *alias* Wright, which had formerly been called the Saracen's Head, while to its north there were the tenements of Symon Oxford and Robert Olyver *alias* Stone. Sir Thomas also sold all the household goods he had at the Angel, apart from some which belonged to John Grymston, gentleman. (Grymston must be the man who, with a colleague called le Grys, obtained on behalf of the Feoffees the Guildhall and other property which had once belonged to the guilds and chantries but had at first been concealed from the Crown Commissioners.) Nicholas Plat sold the Angel and the Castle to William Tassell in 1552.

In 1557, along with a quantity of other land, Tassell conveyed the two inns to the Feoffees to provide money for repairing the parish churches, for setting forth soldiers on behalf of the town, meeting such taxes and other impositions as might be laid on the town and for paying the curates of the town churches. The Feoffees were required to make a special prayer for the good estate of William Tassell during this life and for his soul after his decease in the Common Exhortation of prayer within the parish churches. In 1565 they sold to James Wright, gentleman, a messuage with buildings and ground belonging to the Angel situated between the Angel on the south and a messuage or tenement already belonging to Wright on the north. It abutted on ground forming part of the Angel on the west. The messuage was 19 feet 4 inches long and 15 feet wide, while the ground was 42 feet 4 inches long and 11 feet 10 inches wide at the east end and 15 feet 8 inches wide at the west end.

For reasons which are no longer clear, in 1582 the Feofees alienated the Angel to Robert Potter, and it remained in this family until, in accordance with an order of the Commissioners for Charitable Uses, it was reconveyed to the Feoffees for £100 in 1606. At this date the inn was called the Angel, formerly the Angel and Castle.

As well as providing accommodation for travellers, inns were of great importance in transporting both passengers and goods, for coaches and many goods vehicles plied between inns in various towns. The list of coaches, carts and waggons which served Bury St Edmunds towards the end of the 18th century is included in an early guide to Bury called *A Description of Bury St Edmunds* (1771). For a market town such as Bury St Edmunds the carriers' carts which conveyed goods between the town and surrounding villages must have been of great economic importance, though information about them, other than lists in Directories of the carriers and the inns at which they put up on market day, is hard to find.

As ever, Payne's survey of 1833 provides much information about inns at that date. Although many familiar houses are mentioned here — and some had been built away from the medieval heart of the town, in Kings Road, for example — there were far fewer than there were at the turn of this century. A considerable number still had a brew-house, and presumably brewed their own beer, rather than buying from the common brewers. Many householders will have brewed and sold beer in 'ale-houses' — their own homes — which would not be recorded as inns, to augment the family income; this was a common practice which reached its zenith in the last century. In fact, even in the 17th century, a suit was brought in which the Corporation was accused of allowing over 300 such ale-houses to operate — in a town of less than 5,000 men, women and children. Even in 1887, when Mr Greene and Mr King had amalgamated their breweries, Mr Bishop and his sister still ran the Saracen's Head Brewery and there was a small brewery at the Golden Lion, both in Guildhall Street, as well as Clarke's Risbygate Brewery. A number of houses offered something special in the way of entertainment; the Angel, for instance, had its own Subscription Rooms, presumably the room now known as the Angel Ballroom. Another type of entertainment was offered at the Half Moon, in Butter Market, where Humphrey Steggles, son of William I and brother of William II, had a ten pin ground. There was a bowling green at the Sword in Hand in Southgate Street and a Billiard Room at the Six Bells in Churchgate Street. The Lamb in St John's Street was somewhat unusual in having a butcher's shop, although a number of inns had cow houses or piggeries among their outbuildings. In 1833 the brewers were far from owning a majority of the inns and public houses of the day. Benjamin Greene, for instance, owned only the Dog Tap House in Angel Lane and a beer-house forming part of his brewery in Westgate Street. A number of maltsters, such as Henry Braddock, Mr McLeroth and Robert Maulkin, each owned a number of inns, but in the vast majority of cases, wealthy people from all walks of life had obviously bought one or two inns as an investment.

There have been many changes to the inns and other features of life in Bury St Edmunds. Benjamin Greene's brewery grew, merged with that of Mr King, and gave the town one of its major employers of our own day. In the course of time, many of the inns came into the ownership of this firm, who have cared for the buildings as, according to their lights, people in Bury have cared for buildings over the centuries. It is, perhaps, as typical as anything of Bury that people have so often preferred to adapt an old building rather than build anew. It seems strange to us that Victorian architects should apply fake timbering to genuinely old pubs, but it is in much the same spirit as the Steggles and their contemporaries, who faced old buildings, to try to make them look like the then fashionable stone or stucco-faced buildings. Each generation has added its own contribution to our historic town, some greatly admired, others less so. It all adds up to a very special place, which should be conserved in the light of the factors which have made it what it is today.

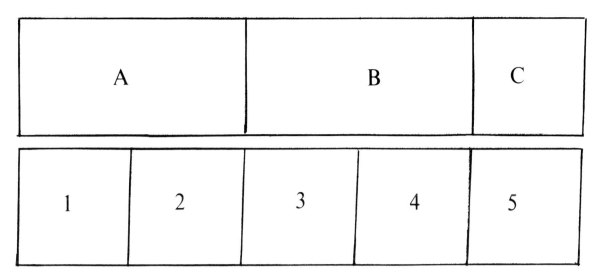

A	B	C

1	2	3	4	5

ABOVE: 1433 rents— A Shop called le Cookree in the rental. The 1417 deed described it as 'le In atte Castell' with a messuage called 'le Cookery'. Robert Cole, butcher, paid the rent of 2s 8d; B Capital messuage with a tenement for which Robert Cole paid 6s 8d, with 8d for the entrance to his tavern under the messuage; both A and B had belonged to Robert of Paston. C Tenement for which John Cote, skinner, paid 2s 2d. CENTRE: 1526 rents: 1 William Holand paid 2s 8d for this which, with 2, appears to be the same as A in 1433; 3 is a head messuage paying 6s 8d which, with a tenement 4, appears to be the same as B in 1433; 5 is identified in this rental as the Angel. Thomas Powle, who paid the rent of 2s 2d also paid 8d for the entrance to a tavern which was said to be between this property and 4. BELOW: Guests arrive at the Angel, c1925. (MS)

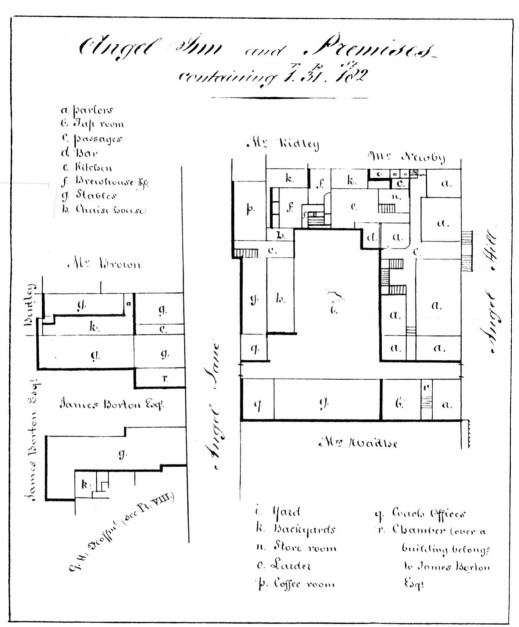

Angel Inn and Premises
containing I. 31. 182

a. parlors
b. Tap room
c. passages
d. Bar
e. Kitchen
f. Brewhouse &c
g. Stables
h. Chaise house

i. Yard
k. Backyards
n. Store room
o. Larder
p. Coffee room
q. Coach Offices
r. Chamber (over a building belong: to James Borton Esq:

Mr Ridley

Mr Newby

Mr Brown

Bartley

James Borton Esq:

C. H. Scotford (see Pl. VIII.)

Angel Lane

Angel Hill

Mr Waithe

Plan of the Angel Inn, which was for many years owned by the Guildhall Feoffees, from J. G. Lenny's plan, 1822. (GFT) OPPOSITE LEFT: Part of the Sacrist's rental, 1526, including the entry relating to the Angel Inn. (StE BC) RIGHT: The Saracen's Head in Guildhall Street, which is now the British Legion Club, photographed before 1916, when it was one of Clarke Bros' houses, and Orbell Fenner was the licensee. (JAW) BELOW: The Suffolk Hotel was formerly known as the Greyhound Inn. It is almost certain that this is the inn which Francis Pynner was authorised to rebuild in 1611, after an older inn on the same site had been destroyed in the fire of 1608. (MS)

LEFT: *The Queen's Head in Churchgate Street is now, like so many buildings in the town, clad in white Suffolk brick. It was formerly a timber-framed building with three gables. The name seems to have been popular, for in 1718 there was a house of this name in Risbygate Street and in 1833 in Eastgate Street. (MS) RIGHT: The Fox in Eastgate Street, a good 15th century building in its own right, is shown here with mock timbering with which some Victorian architect embellished it — it was removed in 1923. (JAW) BELOW: Perhaps this was then the approved style for an old inn, for this photograph of the Dog and Partridge in Crown Street, taken before 1905, shows an identical treatment. (JAW)*

LEFT: By the 1930s, the Dog and Partridge had also lost its superfluous embellishment. (JAW) RIGHT: The Rising Sun in Risbygate Street shows few signs of exterior change. In this view Gifford's baker's shop is on its left; there was a baker's shop there when Payne made his 1833 survey; c1935. (JAW) BELOW: As the Six Bells Inn, the building on the left must have been one of the busiest in 18th century Bury St Edmunds. It became the Masonic Lodge in 1890. On the right is the former Savings Bank, built in 1846. (MS)

ABOVE: The former Sword in Hand Inn, Southgate Street, has been greatly altered since this photograph was taken sometime before 1912. The curved sign depicted an armour-covered arm holding a sword. LEFT: The Bell Temperance Hotel stood where the Job Centre, (in a 1960s building) is now. (JAW) RIGHT: The former Dolphin Inn in Cannon Street had its own brew-house, granary and cow-house in 1833, while the neighbouring land on the town side had a windmill on it. (MS)

LEFT: A 19th century view of the rear of the White Hart in Southgate Street. RIGHT: Cupola House has been a public house for a considerable time, but was built as a residence for Thomas Macro, one of the richest men in the town, in 1694. (MS) BELOW: A view of the Chapel of St Botolph, the remains of which stood at the back of the White Hart; from Yates, Antiquities. (MS)

125

ABOVE: On 22 May 1915, the Bury Free Press reported that the Griffin Hotel on Cornhill had been attacked because it was thought that the landlord, Theodore Jacobus, might be an alien. To the left of the picture can be seen the huge lock which Henshall's the ironmongers used as a trade sign. (JAW) BELOW: Prospect Row appears to have been the first entirely new street to be laid out after the medieval period. All the old houses there have disappeared apart from the former Duke of Wellington public house, now the Jean Corke Day Centre. (MS)

ABOVE: A deed of the Bull in Mustowe, dated 3 October 1502; it stood on Angel Hill, where the Borough Offices are now. The property belonged to John Gardyner, the father of Stephen, who was Bishop of Winchester and became Lord Chancellor under Queen Mary. (SRO(B)) BELOW: The east side of Angel Hill, early this century, shows the One Bull Inn, Burrells' Garage and Warrells' Stores.

SELECT BIBLIOGRAPHY

The literature on Bury St Edmunds is extensive and new titles appear frequently. The Bury St Edmunds section of A. V. Steward's *A Suffolk Bibliography* (Suffolk Records Society, 1979 is recommended as a starting point.

Brakelond, Jocelin of, *Chronicle of Jocelin of Brakelond,* ed. by H. E. Butler (1949). This edition has both Latin text and an English translation.

Chronicle of the Abbey of Bury St Edmunds, translated by Diana Greenway and Jane Sayers, (Oxofrd, The World's Classics, 1989) is a new translation, readily available.

Catlin and Ranson, *The "Jubilee" History of Bury St Edmunds* (Bury St Edmunds, 1887)

Davis, R. H. C., *The Kalendar of Abbot Samson of Bury St Edmunds and related documents* (1954)

Douglas, D. C., *Feudal Documents from the Abbey of St Edmunds at Bury* (Oxford, 1932)

Dymond, David and Martin, Edward (eds.) *An Historical Atlas of Suffolk* (Ipswich, 1988)

Elliott, R. W., *The Story of King Edward VI School, Bury St Edmunds* (Bury St Edmunds, 1963)

Fiske, Jane (ed.), *The Oakes Diaries; Business, Politics and the Family in Bury St Edmunds 1778-1827,* 2 vols. (Suffolk Records Society XXXII and XXXIII, 1990 and 1991)

Gillingwater, Edmund, *An Historical and Descriptive Account of Bury St Edmunds* (St Edmundsbury, 1804)

Gransden , A., ed. *Chronicle of Bury St Edmunds, 1212-1301* (1964)

  'Baldwin, Abbot of Bury St Edmunds', *Proceedings of the Battle Conference on Anglo-Norman Studies,* IV, (1981)

  'The legends and traditions concerning the origins of the Abbey of Bury St Edmunds', *The English Historical Review,* No. CCCXCIV, January 1985

James, M. R., *On the Abbey of St Edmund at Bury* (Cambridge, 1895)

Lobel, M. D., *The Borough of Bury St Edmund's: A study in the Government and Development of a Monastic Town* (Oxford, 1935)

MacCullough, Diarmaid, *Suffolk and the Tudors: Politics and religion in an English County 1550-1600* (Oxford, 1986)

Moore, Ellen Wedemeyer, *The Fairs of Medieval England, An Introductory Study,* (Pontifical Institute of Medieval Studies, Studies and Texts, LXXII (Toronto, 1985))

Proceedings of the Suffolk Institute of Archaeology (1848-date), especially

  Gilyard-Beer, R. 'The Eastern Arm of the Abbey Church at Bury St Edmunds', XXXI (1970)

  L. J. Redstone; "First Ministers Account" of the possessions of the Abbey of St. Edmund; XIII (1907/1909)

  V. B. Redstone, 'St Edmunds and town rental for 1295' XIII (1908)

  S. E. West, 'Excavation of the town defences at Tayfen Road, Bury St Edmunds, 1968' XXXII (1970/72)

Scarfe, Norman *The Suffolk Landscape* (Bury St Edmunds, 1987)

Tymms, Samuel,

  Historie of the Church of St Marie Bury St Edmunds (Bury St Edmunds 1854)

  (ed.) *Wills and Inventories from the Registers of the Commissary of Bury St Edmunds and the Archdeacon of Sudbury* (Camden Society 1850)

  with additions by J. R. Thompson, *A Handbook of Bury St Edmunds* (1891)

Whittingham, A. B., 'Bury St Edmunds Abbey: the Plan, Design and Development of the Church and Monastic Buildings' *Archaeological Journal* CVIII (1951)

Yates, Richard, *An illustration of the Monastic History and Antiquities of the Town and Abbey of St Edmunds's Bury* (1803)

ORIGINAL SOURCES

Without the collections of the Suffolk Record Office (Bury St Edmunds Branch), a book such as this would not have been possible, although, of course, it has been augmented by material in other repositories. The archives of the St Edmundsbury Borough Council, the Guildhall Feoffees and the wills proved in the Sacrist's court, before the dissolution, and in the court of the Commissary of Bury St Edmunds, after the dissolution, have been extensively used. In a book like this, one does not give reference, but I hope I have provided clues to the sources of information wherever possible.

Appendix

Land in the town fields held by obedientiaries of the Abbey, 1295

EAST FIELD	acres
Cellarer	142
Hospitaller (N. Ward)	5
St Nicholas Hospital*	53
Office of Butter	28
	228

SOUTH FIELD†	
Cellarer	31
Almoner	16
Maison Dieu	30
1st and 2nd Wents	
Almoner	28
Sacrist	51½
Third Went	
Almoner	55
Fourth Went	
Cellarer	135
Sacrist	17
	363½

WEST FIELD	
Cellarer	46

RISBYGATE FIELD	
St Peter's Hosptial	20
Total	657½

*As explained in the text, some of this land could be in the South Field.
†No acreage is given for Hardwick Wood and Heath which belonged to the Cellarer or for the Sacrist's woods called Eastlee and Southlee.

Holdings of land in the town fields of the obedientiaries of the Abbey, 1340

Hospital of St Nicholas	44
Hospital of St Saviour	50
Hospital of St Peter	20
Hospital of St John	12
John Costyn for his office	14
Richard Osbern for his office	14
Robert of Thorndon for his office	14
Nicholas of Denham for his office	14
Peter of Harling for his office	14
Master James, clerk, for his office	8
Robert of Cotenhawe for his office	8
Lyon' le Cu for his office	4
Hugo le Harpour	6
Cellarer	440½
Sacrist	80
Almoner	87
Total	829½

It therefore seems that either the woodland is included in the 1340 acreage or a modest addition had been made to the Abbey's holdings between 1295 and 1340. Many of the townsmen who held land would, no doubt, be exempt from the tax, but other taxpayers in 1340 had holdings amounting to more than 833 acres.

Obedientiaries' Holdings, 1295

	Almoner	Cellarer	Chamberlain	Cook	Guest Master	Hospitaller	Infirmarian	Master of the Lady Chapel	Pittancer	Precentor	Prior	Sacrist	Hospital of St John, commonly called Maison Dieu	Hospital of St Nicholas	Hospital of St Peter	Total
West Ward																
Guildhall Street					1	1		2				7				11
Hatter Street								1				6				7
Whiting Street								1				3		1	1	6
Barnwell Street												5				5
Westgate Street												4				4
																33
Risbygate Ward																
Barbour Row								4				6				10
Bater Street	1								2	4		2				9
Brakelond							2			1		5		1	3	12
Brentgovil Street												3				3
Cheese Market							2					1				3
Ironmongers Row	4											9				13
Mustowe												3				3
Neete Market												5				5
Old Baxter Street					3				1							4
Poultry Row		2														2
Risbygate Street		5										2			5	12
Skinner Street												9				9
Well Street									1							1
Woolhill															1	1
																82
East Ward																
Eastgate Street		13						1		2		4	19		1	40
Mustowe	4				1	7	2		1							15
																55
South Ward																
Glover's Row					5		7				4	5				21
Horsemarket												6				6
Maidwater Street					1						1	1				3
Punch Lane												3				3
Raingate Street												5			1	6
Schoolhall Street	2											3				5
Smith's Row					8				4			4		1		17
Southgate Street	8	3	3			1			3	1		7	2			28
Sparhawk Street			1	1								5				7
Yoxfore Lane		1		1					2			5				9
																105
North Ward																
Brakelond	2				1			1				1				5
Burmans Lane												1		4		5
Garland Street	1													2		3
Lt Brackland						1						1				2
Northgate Street		3				3	1					3				10
Scoron Lane	1						2		1							4
																29

130

INDEX

131

SUBSCRIBERS

Presentation Copies

1 St Edmundsbury Borough Council
2 Suffolk County Council
3 Bury St Edmunds Central Library
4 Suffolk Record Office
5 St Edmundsbury Museum Service
6 The Very Reverend Raymond Furnell, Provost of St Edmundsbury
7 HRH The Duke of Gloucester

8 Margaret Statham
9 Clive & Carolyn Birch
10 Henry Rose
11 Roy Ernest Porter
12 L.H.E. Payne
13 Dennis J. Musk
14 Mrs C.D. Penny
15 Rev N. MacCulloch
16 John Marshall
17 Mabel L. Musk
18 Canon & Mrs Richard Norburn
19 Gerald Travers
20 Mrs B.M. Plumridge
21 Robin & Tricia Venn
22 Michael Tupling
23 P.R. Hart
24 Mary Proctor
25 F.G. & M.K. Presswell
26 E.J. Raison
27 Roy Walter James Napier
28 Philip Syrett
29 R. Gale
30 Leslie K. Goodfellow
31 Trevor J. Goodfellow
32 Neville J. Pearson
33 D.A. Rees
34 Michael Ames
35· Mr & Mrs J.P. Growse
36 Margaret Greenway
37 R.G.C. Freeman
38 John W. Fryer
39 David A. Sherlock
40 Eric Flack
41 Betty Milburn
42 P.L.A. McLaine
43 G.D. Wiffen
44 D.M. Sargeant
45 Mrs G. Rhodes
46 Mrs Sandie Taylor
47 D. Taylor Smith
48 David S. Ridgeon

49 Margaret Thelma Holland
50 Mrs Karen Rabett
51 Mrs M.E. Garrod
52 M.R. McAndrew
53 C.J. Pankhurst
54 Mrs William Simpson
55 A.B. Ferguson
56 Mrs Geraldine Jennings
57 C.V.F. Hawkins
58 Mrs B.J. Hill
59 Elsie F. Turvey
60 R. Furnell
61 Louise Higham
62 A.K. Robertson
63 Charles William Gibson
64 Mrs Jill E. Staplehurst
65 R. Rudge
66 Mrs V. Hanaway
67 Mrs E.E. Pryke
68 M.D. Fulcher
69 P.J. Fulcher
70 T.C. Gilchrist
71 Dr Anne Nicholls
72 Sandra Stevens
73 Olive Pointer
74 Elizabeth M. Attree
75 D.C. Tennat
76 Beryl I. Sims
77 H. Glasswell
78 Mrs. M. Leggett
79 Sylvia Colman
80 Mrs Peggy Clarry
81 Elizabeth J. Jansch
82 Mrs D.H. Hodge
83 Neville Blackburne
84 Mrs Annette Tibble
85 Linda Rosemary Cardy
86 J.N.B. Ashton
87 G.W.P. Abel
88 John Wanless Dickson
89 C.B. Day

90 David Cory
91 D.S. Chrispin
92 Noel Stow
93 Bernard R.P. Siffleet
94 I. Sayers
95 Mrs M.L. Hooson
96 Mrs A.L. Pettitt
97 H.L. Howcutt
98 Leslie Harold Lambert
99 R.H. Hempstead
100 Graham J. Bonson
101 Lindsay Dashper
102 Margaret Fayers
103 Gloria J. Abbott
104 Pamela J. Bacon
105 Robert V. Matthews
106 Frank Whitnall
107 Mrs D. Copping
108 Mrs Jan Emerson
109 Mrs J. Heard
110 C.R. Williams
111 Mrs B.M. Hannay
112 Mrs A.M. Honeybourne
113 Daniel Wise
114 Jessica Wise
115 Air Marshal Sir Reginald and Lady Harland
116 G. Moore
117 Mrs M. Cooper
118 S.A. Thompson
119 R. Ceurstemont
120 Miss M. Baker
121 V.J. Bevan
122 Jean Patterson
123 J.R. Bentley
124 W.D. Murrell
125 L.J. Button
126 K.W.J. Marshall
127 Russell Holtaway
128 Mrs M.L. Rogers
129 Mr & Mrs Paul Scarlett
130 Mr & Mrs J.E. Chostner

131 Mrs R. Milner
132 Mrs A. Edgar
133 Joanne Gray
134 Christine Kreckler
135 L.H. Yallop
136 Raie Wilman
137 Mrs M. Kitchingham
138 Sue Walker
139 Mrs Kay D. Nunn
140 Mrs Anne Prasad
141 D. Brooks
142 Mrs R. Payne
143 Mrs E.M. Jacobs
144 Mrs J. Longham
145 Dr David Salt
146 E. Temple
147 J. Brabrook
148 Mrs M.A. Thomas
149 N.P. Moyle
150 P.V. Standard
151 R.H.N. Ambrose
152 Merelina Mary Phyllis MacRae
153 C.F. Taylor
154 Mr & Mrs M.C. Parnell
155 Leicester University Library
156 M. Altuccini
157 Arthur John Adkins
158 Stephen Davies
159 Francis G. Coping
160 A.T. Copsey
161 Miss Susan Over
162 D.R.L. Over
163 Mrs M.B. Lovegrove
164 Amanda J.E. Arrowsmith
165 Nicholas Edward Stevens
166 Robert & Jane Houlton Hart
167 F.S. Jepson
168 Jane Fiske
169 Mrs H.K. Pope

170 Mrs Anne D. Birkby
171 Betty Thompson
172-174 G.V. & A.E. Birkby
175 B.H. Arbon
176 Myrtle Wells
177 Norfolk Library & Information Service
178 Adrian John Purkiss
179 F.C. Smith
180 Tony Williams
181 S.R.K. Taylor
182 Maxine Irving
183 Michael Veale
184 Eric Arthur Graves
185-186 G.R.H. Isard
187 B.O. Tickner
188 John Fry
189 D.J. Forsdyke
190 Mark Woods
191 Mrs S. Soper
192 Stephen Cook
193 Mrs W.M.M. Leftwich
194 M.R. Leftwich
195 A.D. Baynes-Cope
196 Andrew J.R. Budden
197 Mrs A.M. Fayers
198 Joan & Tony Pybus
199 Mr & Mrs A.R. Scarlett
200 Miss J.M. Coleman
201 Miss K.M. Wilkinson
202 Miss H.C. Statham
203 Stanley J. Hunter
204 Dr Colin M. Dring
205 John Entwisle
206 Nigel M. Hale
207 Mark A.F. White
208-209 Ann Johnson
210 P.G. Benford
211 U. Wickett
212 B. Farr
213 P.G. Wood
214 Mrs M.H. Watson
215 Col N.J. Wilson OBE DL
216 Brian Woodall
217 Mrs Jean Blowers
218 Derek B. Bartlett
219 David A. Bartlett

220 A.B. White
221 Leslie N. Bridges
222 J.C. Wolton
223 D.V. Bloomfield
224 P. Vaughan-Williams
225 K.C. Brown
226 C.C. & J.C. Hanson
227 T.J. Whittingdale
228 Julian A.C. Wood
229 Edward Wortley
230 L. Gordon Ward
231 Ruth Donnocker
232 Dr Monica Barnett
233 J.H. Whitfield
234 Rev Michael C. Booker
235 J.A. Twelvetree
236 Mrs. B.M. Blake
237 J.A. Bird
238 Hugh E. Godfrey
239 Eric Flack
240 David Mansfield
241 John Richard Stannard
242 Heather Bennett
243 Mr & Mrs G. Nixon
244 Mrs Alice Esders
245-248 J.A. Wakerley
249 J.D. Woodhead
250 A.W. Buckland
251 Mr & Mrs A.J. Redman
252 John Wilkinson
253 John Knight
254 Sir Graham & Lady Macmillan
255 Lt Col Alistair H.M. Macmillan
256 Mrs Janie E. Elliott
257 Miss Catriona M. Macmillan
258 Donald R.G. Macmillan
259 Butterworth & Son
260 Major & Mrs J.P. Growse
261 Sir Clive & Lady Rose
262 Canon F.W. Fuller
263 Mrs A. Hope
264 Mrs S.A Kiddy
265 Mr & Mrs David Cockram
266

267 Canon John Hasted
268 Peter F. Welstand
269 Dr P.D. Simmons
270 R.G.C. Freeman
271 Peter Wolton
272 Mrs William Simpson
273 Caroline Mackley
274 Stephen Dart
275 M.F. Brundle
276 Walter Bissett Clelland
277 Margarita Livall
278 Mrs W.J. Gagen
279 Gail McMurray Gibson
280 B.H. Christmas
281 Margaret Greenway
282 M. Eileen Clarke
283 M. Green
284 Mrs J. Long
285 G.K. Loveless
286 P. Marchant
287 J. Sansom
288 Mrs S. Younger
289 H.M. Rose
290 A.R. Parkinson
291 D. Brooks
292 A. Spence
293 Pam Howard
294 Alan Jary
295 Gill & Andrew Barton
296 William Jennings
297 Sidney John Trumpess
298 Guildhall Feoffment School
299 J.C. Housez
300 Elizabeth Deacon
301 Lady Gibberd
302 Mr & Mrs M.C. Dunn
303 Brian Roy Reeman
304 Anne Davies
305 St Edmundsbury Borough Council
306 Dr C.B. Boothby
307 The Ven R. and Mrs Garrard
308 Paul Smith
309 Mrs J.M. Pratt
310 Maurice Newton Gandy
311 Mrs Peggy Seeley
312 Cecile & Colin Day
313 Charles M. Slater
314 Allen W.H. Newman

315 Chris Mycock
316 E. Wortley
317 Euan N. Allen
318 Peggy Field
319 Moyse's Hall Museum
320 A.W. Ware
321 Jeremy P. Allen
322 K.J. Burroughs
323 Jenny Carlile
324 St Edmundsbury Borough Council
325 Anne Hope
326 Mr & Mrs P.R. Harrison
327 Virginia Barnes
328 H.A. Cullen MBE
329 Mrs M. Duncan
330 Andrew John Hinchley
331 Sheila Keeley
332 Jean Booth
333 Mrs Edna A. Coote
334 Mrs M.P. Clarke
335 Terence E. Smith
336 Mr P.M. & Dr C.B.E. Rowntree
337 Wendy Mears
338 R.W.M. Clouston
339 Robert Matthews
340 N. Garnham
341 Lawford B.A. Smith
342 C.W. Gibson
343 David Rochford
344 Jane Yallop
345 Anthony W. Ware
346 Roger Avis
347 Elizabeth Parker
348 Mrs K.I.H. Whatley
349 H.W.R. Payling
350 B.J. Phillips
351 G.J. Stacey
352 Clive R. Paine
353 Dr Lucy Joan Slater
354 Lesley Robinson
355 J. Bailey
356 R.R.A. Hearth-Arthur
357 Jenny Stacey
358 Sir Clive & Lady Rose
359-369 Bury St Edmunds Library
370 Monica Place

Remaining names unlisted

END PAPERS: Map of Bury St Edmunds by Richard Payne, 1834, (SRO(B)) FRONT: In part; BACK: Overall.